# Finding the Boy Inside

*Overcoming the Effects of Being Bullied*
*Through the Use of God's Gift*

David A. Klee, Sr., DMA

With Contributions by
Julia W. Klee, MS (Judi)

Inspiration Ministry
Sac City, Iowa

Finding the Boy Inside
*Overcoming the Effects of Being Bullied
Through the Use of God's Gift*

David A. Klee, Sr., DMA
With Contributions by Julia W. Klee
Inspiration Ministry
www.InspirationMinistry.com

Book design by Dr. David A. Klee, Sr. and Julia W. Klee
Published, printed and bound in the United States of America.

ISBN-10: 0692245553
ISBN-13: 978-0692245552 (Inspiration Ministry)

9 8 7 6 5 4 3 2 1

# Dedication

This book is dedicated to all the people who befriended me through my life's struggles and helped me to turn my life around. I would like to especially thank my precious wife, Judi, and my two sons, David and Michael for supporting me along my journey. Thank you!

# Acknowledgements

I would like to thank Sue Davis for her time and help in previewing this book before being released. Your efforts were extremely helpful and deeply appreciated!

# Contents

# Introduction

An untold number of people have been or are being bullied — treated with hostile, relentless, brutal acts specifically targeted toward them without provocation. Bullying ranges from verbal and emotional attacks to harsh physical torment. It is limited only by the aggressor's imagination. This happens to children, teens, and even adults. It happens everywhere: in classrooms, on playgrounds, in physical education classes, in sports events, on the playground, while walking to or from school, in e-mails, in text messages, on the phone, at the workplace, in the military, in nursing homes, and elsewhere. Bullying can literally take place anywhere, anytime. Furthermore, *anyone* can be targeted for torment. It has been speculated that bullying is the most prevalent crime in America today ("Why do People Bully?").

The psychological effects of being bullied are serious and seemingly endless. Victims are often left with lifelong emotional trauma that can lead to mental disorders, missed diagnoses, depression and anxiety, post-traumatic stress disorder (PTSD), attention deficit disorder (ADD) or attention deficit hyperactivity disorder (ADHD), low self-esteem, poor performance in school, eating and sleeping disorders, and lost interest in favored activities. It can be so pervasive as to apparently cause murder rampages for retaliation and suicide. There are countless adults today who have been victimized as children who are carrying lifelong emotional baggage they can't seem to overcome. Despite endless therapy sessions, mind-altering prescription drugs, group counseling, and who knows what, victims still carry the psychological effects of the brutal attacks they endured in their early years.

Those who are targeted are innocent victims. They have done nothing wrong, nor have they invited the attacks. Although literally anyone can fall prey to a bully, victims often share some common traits. They are wonderful human beings, deserving of all the respect anyone is due. Yet, they may have some physical difference, emotional trait, intelligence level, special ability or disability, possessions, religious or cultural belief, sexual orientation, number of friends (or lack thereof), or talent that makes the bully perceive them as being vulnerable targets. However, any problem that sparks the bullying, ultimately stems from the bully, not the victim. If the victim initially reacts by being visibly frightened, crying, running, or not defending him- or herself in a certain way, the bully interprets that as an invitation to continue bullying the person and even intensify the abuse.

Bullies come in all ages, income brackets, genders, races, professions, and cultures. Why do they torment people? Although there are *many* reasons why people bully, there seems to be one underlying common factor — bullies had troubled childhoods where their emotional needs went unfulfilled. They were abused in some way, be it physical and/or emotional. Many times, bullies come from troubled families that lack warmth, love, and shared feelings. They often come from single-parent homes and did not receive the attention they needed as children. There may have been harsh discipline within the family that left them feeling rejected by those who should love them. That makes them more prone to extend that rejection and need for attention onward toward others. It was once thought that generally, even though they don't display it outwardly, bullies may have negative feelings about themselves and pick on those who appear to be vulnerable to make themselves feel better and powerful. This may be the case with some bullies, but more recent evidence shows that many bullies actually have high self-esteem and a sense of superiority, and lack of compassion and empathy toward others. Nevertheless, however they feel inside, their experiences from poor parenting seem to be the root cause of their behavior (Averill).

To compensate for their disturbed childhoods, bullies often have a strong need to be in control and dominate over others. They are driven by their need for power and they enjoy being able to subdue others. They receive positive reinforcement when they bully others, which fuels their behavior. Their "rewards" may come in the form of tangible things like money that they forcibly take from their victims, and material possessions relinquished out of fear by their victims. More powerful intangible rewards are also gained by bullies, such as increased status and prestige they feel from the fact that others fear them. They thrive on the attention they gain by their actions.

Bullying is a serious issue and it does not have to happen. Today we have a heightened awareness of the problem, and society has implemented ways to help stop bullying. However, it takes each and every person to make existing bullying known to proper authorities so actions can be taken to stop it. It takes parents to properly train their children and give them the love and attention they deserve. It takes witnesses to speak up and make the problems known to proper authorities and not turn their backs on the victims out of fear. It takes us all working together to stop this horrendous torment that happens all too often.

The awareness and anti-bullying campaigns that we have today did not exist when I was a child. Many, *many* adults today are living with the consequences of having been bullied as children. They are struggling to overcome the effects of their trauma and are reaching out for help. It is through *my* story that I hope to help others — those victims struggling to find their place in life.

God has a plan in mind for each of us as we're created. He plants special gifts in us that He envisions our using during our lifetime. We're placed in situations to help nurture and develop those gifts, and these situations mold us into what we become as adults. As people, we are products of our environment. Sometimes our environments while growing up are pleasant and nurturing, and sometimes they're not. Nevertheless, as hard as it is to understand, God has reasons for our experiences. These experiences help us to develop into what we become as adults. If we reflect on our past, we can often see God's hand in our lives, find His purpose for our experiences, recognize the gifts He has shared with us, and see His divine plan for our lives.

This book is about my life, from very troubled early years into adulthood, and the discoveries I've made about God's plan for me. Keep reading to learn about my story and how I overcame the horrid effects of extreme bullying when I was a child, through the use of my God-given gift.

If you're confused about God's plan for you, why you exist, why you've been hurt so many times and how to deal with it, then read on. Somewhere, somehow, you'll find God's ultimate plan for you. Look inward as you read my story and think about what God had in mind for YOU when you were created.

Dr. David A. Klee, Sr.

# SECTION I
# My Early Years

# Chapter 1
# In the Beginning

### *Born in Indianapolis, Indiana*

I entered this world six to eight weeks premature. Immediately after I was delivered I had many complications and was not expected to live. The doctors told my mother that I would probably be dead before she could even formally name me. They called in the hospital chaplain to console my family. My mother, who was only seventeen at the time, refused to give in and still wanted to give me a name. She talked to the chaplain and he suggested that she randomly open the Bible he handed her. After she did that, she was asked to point to a random place on a page. Once she did that, the chaplain said that she should name the child the name she was pointing to. I was named "David" after the Hebrew king. The next morning everyone was anticipating arranging a funeral. Instead, I was kicking and screaming and ready to go home. Unfortunately, I did not get to go home for months. But nevertheless, I survived.

Even after I was finally brought home, I was in and out of hospitals almost continuously with many health issues. Not long after I was born, I was joined by two more biological brothers (not twins). The three of us were only a year and a half apart in age. We were ALL premature. For five months of the year, my middle brother and I are even the same age! Overall, my two brothers always seemed to be very healthy.

### *The Move to Florida*

For the first six years of my life, we lived in Indianapolis. Most of my relatives lived in the same area. It seemed like my parents were constantly running me back and forth between doctors and hospitals. Because of my general health problems, doctors suggested that my health might improve if the family moved to a warmer climate. My grandparents had recently moved to Florida. So after some discussion, the decision was made to move. We went to Sarasota, Florida. We lived fifteen minutes from some of the most beautiful beaches in America. Moving south *did* improve my overall health. I remember many joyous days with my family playing in the water at the beach, or fishing with my dad or grandfather. We lived there for one year.

My father had been an electronics engineer for the telephone company in Indianapolis, but in Sarasota, he could only find work at an electronics repair shop. After a few months he was able to get a job in Tampa. He drove an hour and a half back and forth every day for a year. We then moved to Tampa so my dad could be closer to his job at the telephone company.

My parents purchased a new house on the north side of Tampa. This area was growing very fast with numerous new subdivisions. Living in a subdivision was a new experience for all of us. Each area contained a *huge* number of homes seemingly only a few feet apart. It was a lot like living in row houses in a large northeastern city.

## *Realizing I Was Different*

We found out by living in Florida, that most people there do not wear many clothes because of the tropical weather. Like most children, I typically wore only shorts, a tank top, and flip-flops while playing outside, visiting the mall, or shopping. Because of that, it was very apparent how thin I was, and my other deformities could easily be seen. My mother often walked us through the neighborhoods as we were getting used to our new surroundings. That is when I began to notice, even at that young age, that people often stared at me as we walked by. They would point and then softly talk to each other as they were looking at me. Some of them would even shake their head, as if in disbelief at what they saw. Even being as young as I was, I began to realize that I was different. Something was wrong with me.

After a year or two in our new home, my parents had an in-ground pool installed. We all loved it. I swam almost every day while growing up. What I did not realize at the time was how much all that swimming would help me as a professional musician later in my life. My dad even helped my brothers and me build a tree house in our back yard. It was only one foot off the ground, since there were no trees in the yard. But, it was large enough for five to ten children. We enjoyed many hours playing in it. Growing up with my family was good!

# Chapter 2
# My Elementary School Years and
# Getting to Know the "Hoods"

As with most young children, the main focus of my early life was my family. I grew up with two younger biological brothers and a much younger sister who my parents adopted when I was fifteen. Throughout those years I was very frail, small in stature and very underweight. At that time no one knew that I had serious heart problems as well as other health issues brought on by being born prematurely. Also, though it had not been formally diagnosed, doctors were convinced that I had contracted rheumatic fever before I was a year old. Such a condition often leaves people with heart abnormalities.

## *Deformities and Heart Issues*

I wasn't diagnosed until well into my adult years that I suffered from heart arrhythmia due to atrial fibrillation. It is assumed that I was born with this condition. Heart arrhythmia occurs when the electrical impulses that stimulate and coordinate the heartbeats don't work properly. The heart may beat too fast, too slow or irregularly. In my case, it would beat too fast and/or irregularly. During atrial fibrillation, the upper chambers of the heart (the atria) quiver (or beat irregularly) and are unable to adequately move blood into the lower chambers, the ventricles. This situation increases the risk of blood clotting, which in turn, increases the risk of stroke or heart failure. It's a very serious condition that is potentially life-threatening. Symptoms include but are not limited to a "fluttering" feeling in the chest, a racing (or slow) heartbeat, and shortness of breath, lightheadedness, dizziness, and fainting or near fainting. This condition affected my ability to enjoy typical childhood activities.

Being a boy with two brothers and a father who loved sports, I enjoyed sports with my family. We spent endless hours after school and on weekends playing whatever the sport was for the season. I tried to keep up, but usually collapsed after playing. Because of my physical deformities, heart arrhythmia, and other health issues, trying to live and act as a normal child was limited, if not almost impossible. I usually collapsed when I got home after playing sandlot sports.

I was always very thin although I ate like a horse. Despite that, I could never gain any weight. My mother took me to doctors several times over it. She always got the same answer that since I was born prematurely the tendency for me to be thin would stay with me. She was told not to worry about it as long as I was eating well. Because I was so thin, folks often told me (and my parents) that I looked like I had just come from a concentration camp. More than once, the school administrators threatened to look into child abuse against my parents. They assumed I was not getting proper nutrition because of how thin I was. Many times my parents were called in for conferences over my weight and size. A lot of these discussions took place in front of me. I suppose the school administrators did not think I would understand what they were talking about. However, I understood EVERY word! Because of the way everybody treated me, I was convinced that I WAS retarded or something like that. Consequently, I never tried to excel in school.

## Target for Destruction

Because of my small stature, physical deformities and frailness, in elementary school I became fair game for the larger boys — the "hoods" as I came to call them. These were boys who were bigger and older than usual for their grade in school. They had failed an untold number of grades, so they used their size as a means to dominate others. I was constantly singled out, picked on and abused by them. As far as I know, neither of my two brothers experienced the same emotional and physical abuse that I encountered while growing up. I tried not to tell my brothers because I did not want to upset them. My middle brother was actually a lot larger than me and could stand up for himself and fight back when he was picked on. From the beginning of my school years through early high school, my only real companions were my brothers and two neighborhood friends.

In elementary school the "hoods" always targeted me and used me as their patsy for whatever they wanted at the moment. When we lined up for gym class, lunch, or anything else, I was fair game to be verbally or physically abused by them. They often came up to me from behind and pushed me out of the way or elbowed me in the side to get me to move. Another tactic was to use "games" to fleece me of my lunch money or other personal items. More than once if one of the "hoods" liked an article of clothing I was wearing he would "purchase it" from me (whether or not I wanted to "sell" it) for just a few cents. Other times they would tell me that they had something they wanted to "sell" to me. If I refused they would rough me up and threaten me until I bought the item. Numerous times I would come home without having eaten lunch, but instead I would be carrying their trash that they forced me to buy. If my mother found out she would explode in anger and go to the school demanding I get my money back from them and insisting the administration stop the "hoods" from harassing me. The school administrators did little to nothing to remedy the situation. Of course, whenever the "hoods" found out that I had reported them to the school administrators, they would be absolutely ruthless and merciless in taking their anger out on me. Whenever I tried to fight back they would just beat me more fiercely. When I did fight back and try to punch one of them, they would just laugh at me and then beat me horribly. No matter how hard I tried to hit them I could not hurt them. They were always so much larger than me.

### *Dissociation from Surroundings*

By the time I was in the fourth grade I developed a very special "secret place" I could escape to when I was tormented. It was a place where I could shut out the world as I knew it. This "secret place" was a mental state of mind. I could be staring at the teacher, the wall, or outside a window, but I was really in my "special place." People told me that I would be quietly humming and gently rocking while in a trance-like state. I would go there for hours, especially during school, to escape the horrible torment I was experiencing from teachers, administrators, and students. People could scream at me and I would be totally oblivious to them while I was in my "special place." For the most part, I could not remember anything I had done at school during those times.

Psychologists call this type of behavior a form of dissociation where a child can "detach" him- or herself from the immediate surroundings to avoid either an emotional or physical experience. Dissociation is considered to be a coping or defense mechanism in an effort to master, minimize, or tolerate a situation.

## *Music Entered My Life*

One of the most awkward and sensitive times in my elementary years was when I decided to join the school band in the fourth grade. I wanted to play the flute. I came home from school early that year and told my parents that they were starting a band at school and I wanted to be in it. When my parents asked what instrument I wanted to play they looked perplexed when I told them I wanted to learn the flute. I was drawn to the flute almost obsessively. So they took me to the music store to select an instrument. They tried to persuade me to learn a different instrument. Everyone, including the music store owner considered the flute to be a girl's instrument. I tried different instruments but kept insisting on also trying the flute. After much to-do they handed me a flute. After I got the flute and started to actually get a sound out of it, everyone dropped the idea of my learning a different instrument. That started me on my journey with the flute.

Even in the adult world today, many people still think the flute is a girl's instrument. You can only imagine what torment I went through at THAT time in my life, playing what was perceived to be a girl's instrument. Every time I brought my flute to school, I received very abusive verbal teasing and sometimes even more. It got so bad at times that I had to hide my flute (usually in my desk) or the "hoods" would take it and try to hide it from me. Many times as I got ready to go to band I would find that my flute was missing from my desk. After the teacher had everybody look, the flute would be found usually in the back of the room under some clothes.

Despite the abuse I was suffering from, I decided that I was not going to let the "hoods" win. Even at that young age, I developed a real stubbornness and refused to quit the band. I LOVED band class and I loved playing my music. For some reason, I always felt safe in band. It was my refuge from the relentless torment that rained on me almost daily. Outside of band during school time, I basically shut down mentally to my "special place." Usually, the only time I came out of my dissociation was during band class. The one thing I excelled in was music.

The three positive things I always had in my life were my family, my music, and my faith. No matter how much I was picked on or beat up at school, I knew when I came home, I would be treated like a normal child by my family. I could always talk to my brothers and my parents. My mother played piano. The two of us spent numerous evenings together playing music and making up songs.


## *My Fifth Grade Angel*

By the time I was in the fifth grade I would not talk to anyone at school unless I was absolutely forced to. I was too afraid of being told that I was deformed, weak, and/or stupid. On more than a few occasions the teachers questioned my mother about whether I was mentally fit to be in school. One teacher screamed at my mother during a parent/teacher conference. She told my mother that she thought that I must be mentally retarded and that I needed professional help because I would not look at anybody in the eye nor talk to them. (Today they probably would have labeled me as being autistic.) In her opinion, she felt I should be in a mental institution. She also said that they should arrange for surgery for my deformities and other health problems, or I would be scarred for life. (All of this was being said right in front of me!) My parents did actually take me to see medical specialists about my premature birth deformities, but they were told that medical science at the time could do nothing to correct them.

My fifth grade teacher did try to help me and because of that, she has always held a very special place in my heart. During my last two years in elementary school, a lot of students who lived in North Tampa, including me, were transferred to a newly built elementary school. Each classroom had a wall of glass close to twenty feet long and it extended from the floor to the ceiling, where you could see outside. My teacher decided that the students in the class should decorate the room by painting a mural from one side to the other on the glass wall. We decided to paint an underwater scene complete with all of the fascinating creatures you would find under water.

As usual, I was on the sidelines ready for the anticipated rejection when the teacher approached me and asked me to head up the team to paint the mural. I was stunned! She said I could decide what and how to paint everything. Before I could refuse she handed me some paint and a brush and told me to get to work. Well, needless to say I wasn't sure what to do but I started anyway. As I painted, I came to life. I was enjoying myself more than I had through my entire elementary school years. As it turned out, I became the primary painter for the project. The other students lost interest and gradually faded out of the work. I was charged! The teacher had me painting all day, every day, practically for weeks. I was so engrossed in the project that more than once I missed the school bus and my dad had to come and get me.

What I did not know at the time was that the teacher and my mother had had several meetings about me. The teacher told my mom that the school records showed that I was labeled learning impaired and possibly retarded. When my mother asked the teacher if they had run tests on me to determine such results, she told my mother no, that those were just general assumptions of me based on observation only.

My teacher told my mother, based on *her* observations and dealings with me, that I was perfectly normal and should be treated as such. I just needed some help to come out of my shell. During those visits, my mother had informed my teacher about my love for painting. My mother was an artist, and she and I used to paint together when I was young. That is why the teacher had me work on the mural. The teacher wanted to find something that would interest me to help build my confidence.

After several weeks, I finished the mural. The teacher loved it, the school loved it, and I loved it. The teacher proudly showed off the mural to everyone at school. What that teacher did helped to bring me out of my shell for the rest of the school year. I was starting to come alive and was ready for the sixth grade. She was a blessing, as she would not tolerate any students being picked on or abused in her class. For a while at least, I felt safe and secure in school. Unfortunately, my last year in elementary school did not go as well.

### Sixth Grade Disaster

Being such a young child, I was not always sure of what was going on around me. My sixth grade teacher's behavior seemed odd at times. During that school year, we never took tests and rarely read or studied from our textbooks. She would read to us all day from the Bible. We spent a lot of time outside with extra physical activity time. The teacher seemed to cry a lot and was generally self-absorbed most of the time. Because the teacher was preoccupied so much, the "hoods" had a field day with me. For that entire year, they had complete unobstructed access to me with no interference from the teacher. On more than one occasion between classes, they used my head for a bell by slamming me against the metal poles that supported the outside hallways. Because of the renewed abuse, I slipped back into my hole deeper than I had ever been before. I started to question my own sanity.

It wasn't until the last few weeks of the school year that my teacher's true problems were revealed. She was an alcoholic and was drinking heavily during the school day in the classroom. The administration learned of this and she was fired. They brought in a substitute for the remaining four or five weeks of the school year.

But by then, the damage had been done. We did not learn anything the entire year nor did we have any testing. My sixth grade class had lost an entire year of learning! The school board did not know what to do with us — promote us to seventh grade or hold us back another year. Because of possible lawsuits, they promoted all of us to the seventh grade. Many of my peers failed the next grade, but somehow I managed to pass.

# Chapter 3
# Junior High Hell

Junior high school was probably the worst period of my life. I was picked on and/or beat up probably every day. To make matters even worse, I had to walk each day because we lived within two miles of the school. My father worked nights and was not home until after I had to be in school, and was still asleep when it was time for me to come home. My mother was a stay-at-home mom at the time and did not drive. The whole area of town was made up of giant subdivisions, each comprised of *many* homes. Many of the "hoods" lived in the same area that I did, which meant I had to confront them almost daily while walking to and from school.

I gave up asking the school administrators to help me. After a while they started accusing me of starting the fights or making it all up. I even hated to go to the bathroom because the "hoods" would be there, seemingly waiting for me. Actually, they were in there hiding while they were smoking. If I happened to walk in the boy's room while they were in there, they would throw me around the bathroom, stick my head in the urinals, and slam me against the sinks. I still have the chipped and crooked teeth to show for it. They told me that I had to have my "daily beating" to keep me in line. I was so small in junior high school that I had to put books on the floor for my feet to rest on.

After several months of the torment and daily beatings I often went limp when approached for my next beating. I become like a rag doll until they were finished with me. I realized that fighting them only made it worse, much worse. I would go limp and withdraw into my own world and wait until they were done.

## *A Living Punching Bag*

One day as I was walking home, I spotted one of the "hoods" as I was coming around the last corner before entering the street where I lived. He immediately saw me and chased after me. Eventually he caught me and dragged me back to the middle of the street right in front of my house. Once there, he decided to demonstrate his "superiority" over me by holding both my arms together with one hand, raising me up in the air, and then slapping and beating me with his other hand. This was done right in front of my house and across from where a girl my age lived. Once he was done giving me my "daily lesson of obedience," he dropped me and walked away laughing as I collapsed in the middle of the street crying.

## *PE (Physical Education) Class Torment*

In junior high school, I had gym class every day. I absolutely feared going to PE because of the demands of having to exercise and play sports right beside the "hoods." I was fair game for them—a vehicle for proving their "manliness" to the world. Several times the "hoods" ripped off my gym clothes and paraded me around the girls and boys PE classes to show how skinny I was. Many times when this happened, there were as many as fifty girls and boys watching as I was paraded around. Everybody would be laughing and pointing at me. Many of the girls would say very abusive and offensive things to me. I often saw the same students in the hallways and classes every day. They would point their fingers at me, make crude remarks, and laugh at me. I wished that I could die!

I was rarely selected to play on a team in PE unless the coach forced a team to use me. Even then, I would be stuck in the outfield during baseball, or in the far back area of the football field to stay out of the way. I never liked team sports at school because of the fear of being rejected and not wanted. I hated PE.

In PE during the spring track season, we were lined up to practice the high jump. At that time I did not know that the "hoods" told everybody else not to use the high jump until after I had jumped over the bar. I jumped over the bar and prepared to land on my backside safely onto the saw dust pile on the ground. Instead, when I hit the ground I was knocked out. After what seemed like minutes I regained consciousness with the help of the coach. As I looked around some of the "hoods" were laughing so hard they were falling on the ground. After I got up, the coach removed the saw dust and discovered that someone had buried a cement block in the ground, and then lightly covered it up with the saw dust. The coach was furious and demanded to know who had done that. Of course, no one spoke up. The coach then made everybody run extra laps that day. I went to the hospital with a mild concussion.

If we had to run or do other types of physical exertion sports, I was always the last to finish because of my heart. Even at that age, my heart was going in and out of arrhythmia, although at the time I didn't understand what was happening. The stream of intermittent heart arrhythmia episodes could go on for hours leaving me totally exhausted and worn out. Also, there were other times I would completely collapse on the floor not being able to move because I was so weak. Many times my parents took me to the doctor or hospital in an attempt to figure out the cause of my extreme fatigue. It was to no avail. By the time they would get me to the doctor or hospital the heart would be back in normal rhythm. No one had any idea what was happening to me. Because they did not see me during an arrhythmia event, doctors simply told my parents I was just out of shape or faking it. This scenario followed me well into my adult life.

The worst part of junior high PE class was taking a shower at the end of each session. If the "hoods" caught me in the shower they would often push me around and take turns taunting me about how skinny and deformed I was. I was so small and thin that I did not want them seeing me in my nakedness! I could not understand why God allowed this. I wondered why I had to endure that every day.

### Cars Vandalized

The "hoods" were so intimating that when one of the teachers tried to stand up against them after witnessing an incident, that same teacher found that her car had been turned upside down and dragged around the gravel parking lot. Another teacher's car was set on fire. Incredibly, this was happening in the middle-class area of North Tampa, Florida!

### Hiding the Abuse

I eventually stopped telling my parents about the abuse because I got tired of upsetting them. If I came home with bruises, blood or scratches I tried to hide the injuries. I was even forced to carry some of the "hoods'" books around to their classes and do other errands for them. They loved to show me off to the other "hoods." I was their "boy," their property. Everybody would be laughing at me in the hallways when they saw me. Some of "hoods" even wanted to use me to help them cheat in class on tests. Fortunately, that never worked out because they soon learned that my grades were not much better than theirs.

### The Runaway Girl

One morning an announcement came over the school public address system directing every male student in the school to report to the cafeteria immediately. Once we were there I noticed many policemen, medical personnel, and other officials in coat and tie. They were all very serious in their demeanor as they talked to us. They announced that a runaway girl had set up "shop" in Tampa and was having sex with hundreds of males over a period of several weeks. They went on to say that the girl was infected with several sexually transmittable viruses. Then they wanted anybody who had physical contact with her to remain while everybody else was dismissed. As I left the cafeteria I noticed that numerous male students remained, including almost all of the "hoods."

### Junior High Drum Major

The highlight of my junior high years was playing in the school band. I even was appointed to be the drum major during my last year. Luckily the band director selected the drum major based on skill, not popularity! Back in the "old" days we had junior high schools, not middle schools as they do today, and all school functions were set up like mini high schools. The band marched for halftime shows at football games and we even marched in the Gasparilla Parade.

# Chapter 4
# High School

In Florida at the time, there was no age requirement for attending school like there is today. When I was in junior/senior high school many of the "hoods" were several years older than me. Some were even joining the military services right out of *junior* high school. Many of them had cars or motorcycles and drove themselves to school while in *junior* high! Apparently, they had failed several years and kept repeating the same grade. By high school, those same "hoods" were enormous. They were men, mostly in their late teens to early twenties.

By the time I was a freshman in high school I was ready to quit school. I felt like life was only going to get worse. But with my parents' urging, and my desire to play in the high school band, I forged ahead. (In Tampa, the band programs were fantastic!) I decided to try to alter my strategy on how to keep from getting beat up by the "hoods." I learned where they hung out, where they smoked between classes, the halls they walked in going to and from classes, and even where they parked their cars and motorcycles. I did my best to avoid them. Unfortunately once again, PE class was the worst place I had to deal with them because I had nowhere to hide.


### *More PE Torment*

In PE, the "hoods" would wait for a chance when the coach was not looking so they could abuse me once again. Many times when the coach stepped out for a moment, they would come up to me and hit me or call me abusive names. If I complained to the coach the "hoods" would find me later and beat me up even worse than normal for telling the coach about them.

I always hated taking a shower in PE because of the fear of the "hoods" finding me and physically and/or emotionally abusing me even more. If I tried to leave the shower when they walked in, they would grab me and hold me down and beat on me. Other times they would drag me outside and make me wait until they were finished, often making me late for my next class.

While in high school I became friends with another student who was legally blind. The only way he could read anything was to put the document up so close to his face that it almost touched his nose. His mind made up for what he lacked in eyesight. As far as I was concerned he was a mental genius. Without any kind of mechanical device, he could calculate how many cigarettes it would take butted end to end to go to the moon or a planet, etc. He happened to be in my PE class. Unfortunately, because of his visual impairment, he was also fair game for the "hoods." Many times the "hoods" would take his tennis shoes (or other personal items) out of his locker and set them on the top of his locker or elsewhere in the locker room. Of course everybody else could see where his personal belongings were but he could not. The "hoods" would be nearby literally rolling on the floor while my friend was looking for his shoes. Anybody late for roll call after dressing for PE had to run laps. Because my friend could not find his shoes for several minutes, he was late many times for roll call and was punished for it.

Once I stayed behind to see why he was late so often. That was when I saw what the "hoods" were doing. I was never so mad in my life. But I knew if I tried to help him in front of the "hoods," they would probably kill me. So I waited until later during the PE class to tell him where they were putting his shoes and other personal items. After that, he knew where to look if his things were missing.

I eventually became his official running buddy, since he could not see what was in front of him. I would run beside him and talk to him. By listening to my voice he was able to stay on the track.

### Between Class Fears

The high school I attended in Tampa was very large, with over three thousand students. Between classes there would be a mass of humanity in the hallways — a perfect hiding place for the "hoods" to trap me and inflict their pain. They were able to get away with almost anything. I even tried walking outside the building between classes, to escape their tyranny. This was to no avail, because the school officials would catch me and punish me for being outside.

### Lunchtime Woes

Even at lunch, the "hoods" would find me and take whatever food they wanted off of my tray. Sometimes they would even force me to buy food for them with my own money on the pretense that they would pay me back later. Of course, they never did. Because of that, sometimes I had no money for lunch.

My grandmother worked in the school cafeteria. She arranged for me to have a free lunch every day in exchange for my working fifteen to twenty minutes in the dish washing room during my lunch period. I wasn't very happy about it because I knew the "hoods" would have a lot of fun with that. (Any student who worked in the cafeteria at that time was looked down upon as being poor.) But because my family was paying for three lunches every day for my brothers and me, I agreed. Sure enough, the "hoods" really loved that! When they came up to drop off their dirty trays, they would stand there by the counter and laugh and point at me. They would usually come up and throw their trays at me while laughing! Sometimes there would be a crowd of ten to twenty students, all standing there laughing at me. I wanted to die! I could not understand why I had to suffer and endure that kind of personal agony.

### High School Band Reprieve...Sort Of

When I was in the school band I was able to meet girls. I often fantasized about some of them becoming my girlfriend. I dreamed of how nice it would be to have a normal relationship with girls instead of always hiding within and shutting out the world. Some of the girls became like sisters to me. We remained good friends until their boyfriends found out and would then forbid them to talk to me because I was not "human." Since I was a "freak," the girls had to stay away from me. Once their boyfriends threatened them, the girls would no longer talk to me, or even look at me.

There were only a few "hood-like" students in the high school band. They made every effort to pick on me and tease me as much as they could. I did my best to stay out of their way. I was lucky in that my band director ran the program like it was boot camp (I think he was a World War II veteran). If he saw someone picking on me or anybody else, he would punish the perpetrators by making them do extra work such as marching up and down the football field for an hour. By my second year in the band, most of the band "hoods" left me alone. One of them even offered to help me if I was ever picked on.

### The Halloween Dance

By my senior year of high school, many of the "hoods" had quit school. Because of that, I almost enjoyed my last year of high school even though I never felt totally comfortable, or that I really belonged there. I still felt like I was an outsider. I longed for normal relationships with my peers.

While in high school, the local teen center was sponsoring a Halloween dance where everybody who came to the party was expected to dress up in a costume. I heard about the teen center party from some of the students at school. My mother asked me if I was interested in going. She knew how lonely I was, longing to be with other teens my age. I was so lonely for friendship that I asked my parents if they could drop me off at the teen center and pick me up when it was over. Everyone was supposed to go to the party in disguise and then only later take their mask off. My mother and I decided that I could go as a mummy.

On the evening of the party, I was really excited about the event. My mother helped to apply all the rolls of medical gauze to cover me up completely. Even my face was covered. I only had holes for my eyes and nose. Later, my parents dropped me off at the teen center. I was extremely nervous but excited at the same time. After all, I was actually at a teen event surrounded by peers my age, and nobody was laughing or running away from me. Almost immediately several girls and boys approached me and started talking to me. After several minutes it occurred to me that the reason they were talking to me was that they did not know who I was. They could not see my face. Then I started to get nervous. What would happen if they found out who I was? All of the girls were trying to figure out who I was. I was totally enjoying all of the attention, but scared at the same time! They were naming all the popular boys at the school. Every time I told them that their latest guess was incorrect, more girls would come over and help try to identify who I was. This went on for over an hour until it was time for everyone to unmask themselves. At that point, I did not want to reveal who I was and tried to avoid unmasking, but one of the girls grabbed the gauze on my face and pulled it down. Once she saw who I was, she jumped back in disgust and shrieked. The other girls were equally alarmed! Then they immediately ran from me and began telling everyone else what they discovered. I ran out of the teen center and sat on the curb waiting for my parents while I cried.

### The Damage Was Deep

A few of my peers ignored the threats from the "hoods" and actually talked to me and we became friends. But by then the damage had been done. I was a totally devastated human being with no self-worth, no self-confidence and I wanted to die. I could not understand why God would allow this. The only thing that kept me going was my family, my music, and my faith.

According to psychologists, adults who were abused as children may suffer extreme shyness, embarrassment and feelings of being inferior to others. They don't believe they make mistakes. Instead they believe they *are* mistakes. They feel that no matter what they do, it won't make a difference. They feel they are and always will be worthless and unlovable. That describes how I felt about myself.

I have spent a lifetime trying to "fit in." Even to this day, when I am attending a professional meeting with my colleagues, I feel like I never really fit in. I still have the hardest time with this, usually feeling uncomfortable in gatherings. I feel like I am outside looking in and that no one will hear or care to listen to me. If someone disagrees with anything I say I have a very hard time standing up for my convictions because of my past torment and feelings of hopelessness and helplessness. I feel like no matter what I say or do, I cannot win.

Because of the physical and emotional abuse I suffered all those years in school, my graduating grade point average was a mere 2.0 (C) and I graduated in the 760th place out of 970 students. I did not crack open a book throughout all of my school years, but somehow I still managed to graduate from high school.

### *Arrhythmia Troubles*

When I was in my late teens and early twenties I was always very tired and struggled to keep up with "normal" people. I had to try very hard not to show how I really felt. What I did not know during those years was that my heart was actually in and out of arrhythmia quite a bit. The doctors never detected the heart in arrhythmia when I went to the hospital. Whenever my heart bounced back and forth like that it took days for me to get back to normal. Since my heart was frequently in and out of arrhythmia, I never really felt very good.

When I was in high school I played in the marching/concert band. By the time marching practice was over, I was usually on the verge of total collapse. Somehow I was always able to hide that fact. Most people never knew about my heart problem.

For me, being chronically fatigued was a normal way of life. I did not know what it was like to be "normal." I could fall asleep (and still can because of my medications) at any time. This often gave people the impression I was taking drugs or doing something inappropriate. I have actually had strangers come up to me and ask if something was wrong because of the way I looked and acted as a result of the medications!

## Music Was Part of My Soul

The main focus of my high school years was again, music. Participating in the band is what kept me in school. My high school band was considered one of the finest in Florida at that time. The band program was part of a very large 5-A high school and experienced about thirty years of straight superior ratings at every district and state marching or concert festival. The band was better than a lot of college bands. At the state festivals, we received fifteen minute standing ovations after our performances! It was truly the only reason I stayed in high school.

By the end of my junior year I decided that I wanted to be a musician for life. But to do that, I needed private lessons as part of my preparation. A large percentage of the band students (roughly fifty to seventy-five percent) took private lessons. I had tried for years to convince my parents of the importance of lessons and to allow me to be tutored, but to no avail. Early in my junior year, something inside urged me to try again to ask my parents about lessons. We were what I would call "middle-class poor." My dad worked as an electronic technician for the phone company and I had a stay-at-home mom. We had all our basic needs taken care of but there was little extra money. I offered to help pay for the lessons from my part-time job but needed transportation. This time after talking to my parents they finally decided to get me started on flute lessons. I found out years later that my mom had threatened my dad with a kick in his behind unless he agreed.

## Finally...Flute Lessons

We found a wonderful young woman working on her master's degree in flute performance at the nearby university. I was scared to death to meet her because of fear of rejection. (After all, I was the freak. I was not human.) The moment we met, she put me at ease by always looking at me directly in my eyes instead of looking down at me like so many people did. She talked to me like I was a very special human being. After my first lesson, we both got along very well. She was twenty-five and newly married, and I was seventeen at the time. She turned out to be a great teacher, friend, confidant, and big sister. Likewise, she told me that she saw a great talent inside of me ready to burst out. I just needed to work the hardest I had ever worked in my life to clear away the rough edges. Even though she was my high school flute teacher for just over a year and a half, she had a profound effect on me that has lasted a lifetime. She was the one responsible for turning my life around! After all these years, I can still reflect back and see that she was an angel sent from God to help me.

I estimated I was about five to six years behind most of my musician classmates in musical training. I had some serious catching up to do. For the first time in my life I started working VERY hard. *I had somebody who believed in me!* For the first time I began to feel like I was worth something. I thought that if my flute teacher saw something worthwhile in me then maybe I *was* worth it! I could not believe how fast I progressed. In musical terms, I climbed five to six years up the music ladder in one year.

### *District Solo and Ensemble Festival…*
### *The Beginning of My Turnaround*

At Christmas, my flute teacher helped me to decide what flute solo to play for the Solo and Ensemble Festival scheduled in the spring. When I showed it to my band director he said that it was too contemporary and difficult for me. He said that I could not handle it. After getting home I contacted my flute teacher and told her what my band director said. She got mad and told me that she thought I could play it with a lot of hard work. Because of her, I decided to go ahead and work on it despite what my band director said. And boy did I work! In Florida, not only do you have to learn the solo, but it must be memorized. It was at that time that I began to learn how fast and easily I *could* memorize!

Well, finally the day came for me to perform the solo. I was a nervous wreck. This was the first time I had ever performed something of this level and magnitude. Of course the "demons" inside of me were trying to wreck my performance saying "You're a nothing! You're a freak. Give up! You can never be a success at anything!"

But, because of my parents' and flute teacher's faith in me, I went in and performed to the best of my ability. Later, many of my bandmates ran up to me to tell me they saw the score results on the bulletin board outside the judging room. They told me that I had made a superior rating, the top score I could make. I almost passed out! For the first time in my life I witnessed, for myself, success from my hard work. I immediately called my flute teacher to tell her the wonderful news. We both cried.


### State Solo and Ensemble Festival

In Florida, if you make a superior rating at the district level you are then eligible to go to the state level. My flute teacher immediately started to prepare me for the state performance. I was really "fired up" then. My band director, bandmates, and even relatives began to see me in a different light. I liked it. I liked being thought of as a success, rather than a constant failure. I worked harder than ever before in my life. The state level competition was located on the other side of the state so all of the music students from my school went together on a chartered bus.

Before I left, my flute teacher called me and asked if I could come by to see her. When I went over to her house she said that I had been sounding like a million dollars and she felt that my flute would not do me justice for my upcoming performance. (I had a typical student-line non-professional flute.) She walked over to her table, picked up her Haynes flute (a top-line professional, totally hand-made flute) and handed it to me saying, "You need a flute that will compliment your million dollar performance this weekend." I could not believe it! She loaned me her flute! We both cried some more.

At the state competition once again I had to summon up my inner strength to combat the "demons" trying to convince me that I was still a failure. I went in and performed very well. I was so prepared that there was no way I could not give a superior performance. We had to wait until all performances were completed before any scores were announced. After the results were tallied, my band director ran up to me and informed me that I had just given one of the best performances of the day! I was declared one of the top high school performers in Florida.

# Chapter 5
# My First College Music Audition

In the spring of my senior year of high school, the Shenandoah Conservatory (West Virginia) School of Music Wind Ensemble was touring in Florida. The school is affiliated with the Methodist church. My minister and parents were able to help me set up an audition for a music scholarship from the church for the next school year. After my winning performance at the state Solo and Ensemble Festival, I was pumped up for the audition. I auditioned for the conductor when the Shenandoah Wind Ensemble came to Tampa. About two weeks later I was told that I was awarded a full scholarship to attend the conservatory for the next fall. I was floored! For the first time in my life, I actually felt like somebody! It was a great feeling.

After graduation from high school, I was enjoying my summer and preparing to leave for college when I got a letter from the conservatory. In it, they expressed their regrets that they had to withdraw my scholarship due to lack of funding because of the Viet Nam War. They said that I could still attend, but had to find other means to pay the tuition. This was a private Methodist university and very expensive. I was stunned. I wondered, "What do I do now?" Back in 1968, all men who were not in college could be drafted to fight in Viet Nam. But it was beyond the usual time to enroll in any of the local colleges or universities. My dad got really "fired up" and helped me. He located a private two year Christian college in Tampa that would accept me even as late as it was — nearly August. So instead of going to the conservatory I ended up going to a local two year college with no instrumental music program. But I soon remembered that the University of South Florida was only ten miles away. I found out that I could take classes part-time as a non-degree-seeking student even though it was too late to be admitted as a full-time degree-seeking student. So, I registered for the concert band and flute lessons at the University of South Florida. I told myself I was going to be OK.

### *Audition for Performance Groups*

At the university, I found out that I had to audition to be accepted into their premier wind ensemble performance group. I also found out that there were thirty-five flute majors and some of them were very advanced performance majors. One of them performed in the Florida Symphony. They were incredible musicians. Well, I auditioned and waited patiently for several days before the results were posted. When the results were shown, I discovered that my name was not on the list, and that they only took five flutists. I was devastated. Well, I did the usual — I went home and cried, told my mother, and told my college and high school flute teachers. Both of my flute teachers told me that they thought that I was good enough to be in the premier wind ensemble and suggested that perhaps I just had a bad audition. Well I was starting to feel better but I really wanted to be in the band. Then I got a phone call from my college flute teacher instructing me to go talk to the university band director about my audition. She said that she had called him about it. Boy was I nervous then! I figured that maybe somehow I had opened "a can of worms" and made the band director upset from my complaining. Somehow I managed to gain the strength to go talk to him.

At the time, the band director was also the chairman of the music department. I was absolutely scared to death to go talk to him. After all, who was I to question his decision about the chair placements? It took every ounce of my inner strength to go talk with him.

After I walked into his office I began apologizing for any waves I had caused by complaining about the results of the audition. He told me that there was no problem and he was happy to explain the results of the audition to me. He said that (as I was aware of) there were thirty-five strong flute majors at the school, but he only used five in the premier wind ensemble. The music department was so large, it actually had five other concert bands, two jazz bands, and a symphony orchestra. The five students who were accepted into the band were all senior flute performance majors.

Then he went on to state that the sixth chair, the next position from the audition process, was awarded to me, a freshman! I was sixth overall out of thirty-five flutists! He said that I had given an incredible audition. Then he said that in the spring semester he anticipated one of his flutists to be graduating and that he would probably move me up.

As I walked out the door I was on "Cloud Nine"! I immediately called my high school flute teacher. We both cried! I could not believe how far I had come in one year. And sure enough, I was moved up to the premier wind ensemble the second semester. What I did not know at the time, was that this was only the beginning of my long journey in music.

### *Starting to Pull it All Together*

I never dated in high school because I felt like no girl would ever want to go out with me. In college, I was the only male flutist. Once I got to know some of my fellow flutists, I finally got the nerve to ask some of them out. Testosterone is an amazing chemical, isn't it? To my amazement not one girl ever refused to date me. The funny development from this is, as I moved up in the flute section after each audition, the girls I surpassed refused to go out with me after that! I began to build my male ego slowly by dating.

By the second semester of college I was able to transfer to the university as a full-time degree-seeking student. I was still having difficulties trying to study in my classes. I could not focus very long. As in my previous school years, I still rarely cracked open a book. Somehow I managed to keep a C average in college.

By the time I started college, most of the teasing, taunting, and verbal and physical abuse was history. I was very leery of it starting up again. I still did my best to avoid going anywhere the "hoods" might be and I avoided any of the places where they were known to hang out.

# SECTION II
## Early Adult Years
### *(Starting to Find Myself)*

# Chapter 6
# The Gift of Teaching Music

During the second semester of my freshman year in college, I got a phone call from my high school flute teacher. She was very excited to tell me her husband was just offered a job teaching piano at a small college in Canada. He had been working on his master's degree in piano performance at the University of South Florida. Then she went on to tell me that they would be moving within a month. Before I could congratulate her she then went on to say that I would be getting a series of phone calls within the next few days. She recommended to all of her students that I take over as their flute teacher. I was stunned.

After I thanked her, I hung up the phone and was speechless for a few minutes. I had gone from a worthless nothing to being a flute teacher in a little more than a year. Then the reality *really* hit me. I would be teaching flute lessons to thirteen- to seventeen-year-old girls. I was terrified of being rejected again. I had to do a lot of soul searching to convince myself that I could teach lessons. I was absolutely petrified that I would be rejected by the girls. I had only just recently started dating girls at the university I was attending. I spent many hours in my "special place" trying to think about it and sort it through in my mind. I really did not think I could go through with it. Slowly over a period of several days, I settled down and thought it through and kept telling myself that I could do this. After all, if my former high school flute teacher (and university flute teacher) had *that* kind of confidence in me, then I COULD do it. So I began to teach flute lessons. As it turned out, I was not rejected by any of the young flutists. I soon found my calling — teaching children and young adults the joy of music. I have been teaching flute lessons ever since I was nineteen years old.

# Chapter 7
# Leaving College to Pursue
# Full-Time Performing

I grew up during one of the most violent times in contemporary American history. The Viet Nam War was going full-force during the late 1960s and the early 1970s. At the time, the federal government modified the existing law about the draft. The original draft law stated that all men, after turning eighteen, could be drafted into the military. When the Viet Nam War started, the law was changed so that young men who were going to college could defer being drafted until they completed their collegiate training.

To defer the draft, you had to complete a certain number of college hours a year to remain in-phase. Once a student was out-of-phase, he could be drafted. Another twist to the draft law was that they also initiated a lottery system where the draft board selected letters of the alphabet each year. From this list of letters, they would assign numbers from 1 to 365, representing the days of the year. The higher your "number" the less the chance that you would be drafted once you were out-of-phase or graduated from college.

I was barely holding onto my grades academically and found myself dropping classes if I was struggling in them. Again, I was not studying. I could not focus. After my first year I did not have enough hours to be in-phase, which meant I could be drafted. Sure enough, I was called to have my physical to be drafted into the army. I, along with several male members of my high school graduating class, including several of the "hoods," took a bus trip to Gainesville (Florida) for our army physical. At that time I had a ruptured eardrum from a swimming accident, heart arrhythmia problems, and weighed somewhere around 116 pounds (at five feet, eleven inches), but of course, I still managed to pass their physical. The army sergeant stated as we were loading the bus to go home, that we would be getting our draft papers within the next month. As God was with me, the very next week the federal government had their first draft lottery. The letter "K" was assigned a number of 250, which meant I probably would not be drafted that year. As it turned out, I was never drafted.

### Goodbye College...Hello Music

At that point in my life, I decided to take a break from college. I got a job in downtown Tampa, working in a print shop for a medical company. This allowed me time to pursue commercial music. I was always fascinated with pop/rock bands and wanted to start one myself. About that time I began dabbling with guitar and soon thereafter, my brother, our neighbor, another friend I grew up with, and I put together a band. We started out by playing in Methodist church coffee houses that catered to teens and young adults. These were really popular at the time. Before long, the musical commitments became almost a full-time function between practicing and performing. We were driving all around the state of Florida performing in church teen centers and other similar venues.

It was soon evident that we wanted to make it a full-time endeavor which meant that we would have to look at other opportunities.

### *Playing on a Cruise Ship*

During that time we landed a job on a cruise ship based out of Miami. The ship had five bands and a piano bar. All of the other musicians were from Europe. We were the only American band. As it turned out, we were hired to perform on the ship when many high school and college students were taking their spring break on the cruise. Boy, did I have to grow up very quickly! I was the leader of the group, which meant I had to conduct all the business dealings for the group.

In addition to being the business leader, I also had to keep the band members in line. No one was twenty-one yet. One of the band members was found asleep one morning lying on the pool table on the top deck. Lying alongside of him was a girl, also asleep. Fortunately they were both dressed. I constantly had to go find the drummer when it was time to perform because he was always busy chasing girls.

My brother, the co-lead singer, came down with a bad cold and took an antihistamine pill to help fight the symptoms. When the bartender found out about his cold he offered him some drinks to also help relieve the cold symptoms. Well, with the mixture of the cold medicine and the liquor, my brother started saying things over the microphone that were not exactly presentable to the public. It took a lot of explaining to the ship's captain the next day to prevent us from getting fired.

Our duties included playing music between performances in their show club and entertaining on the top deck when they were having evening pool parties. It was exciting but hard work with my group sometimes playing as late as 3:00AM in the morning and having to be ready to go by 4:00PM the next day.  We were an instant hit because we were the only group that played American top forty music. The club was usually packed with dancers until closing. This was the first time I was around professional musicians from Europe. They were very skilled and reserved. Most of the European musicians were in their forties and fifties. They really did not know how to deal with us young American musicians!

The ship sailed from Miami to Nassau, to Freeport, and then back to Miami each week. We were on the ship for several weeks. At the end of our contract, the cruise line offered us a yearlong contract as well as a recording contract if we agreed to stay on. Two of the band members had girlfriends and wanted to go back home to Tampa, so we politely declined. I wanted to stay. While we were performing on the cruise ship I was treated like an adult and a professional. It was a new and exciting feeling for me. I could have stayed on the cruise ship forever. Overall, we did a good job for the cruise lines.

### Back on the Mainland

After returning, I taught flute lessons at my dad's hardware store. My dad always wanted to be in business for himself. Even though he worked nights for General Telephone and Electronics Corporation (GTE), he was able to start a small business. It was a combination hardware and musical instrument store in North Tampa. Naturally he wanted me to teach my flute lessons there. So one day I was waiting for a flute student to arrive and walked to the front of my dad's store, and I saw her. There was a girl wearing a granny dress with hair past her bottom trying out one of my dad's guitars. I was stunned! As she tried the guitar she also began singing. I instantly fell in love with her voice. Eventually I figured out a way to convince her to sing with my band. We were performing at school dances and needed a female singer for some of the songs.

I discovered from very early on, that I was drawn to Judi through her music. It wasn't long before we started dating. She was in high school and I had just dropped out of college. Even though I was a little older than her, she was (and still is) much more mature than me. It wasn't long before we both realized that we were soul mates.

We had returned from the cruise ship job a few months earlier when I first met Judi. I was instantly extremely attracted to her. I did not know at the time, but she was another young adult who had been scarred from life's woes. She grew up with an abusive father. At first, I hired her to sing in my band. Many of the jobs we had were junior/senior high school dances. We needed a female voice in many of the songs. Even before we were in love we became good friends. I always felt extremely comfortable around her. I never felt like she was looking down at me or judging me in any way. By the time my band was starting to perform full-time in night clubs I realized that I was very in love with Judi and wanted to spend the rest of my life with her. The problem was that I had nothing to offer her but my love. I had no job skills, no education, no money, and no security — only my unabashed love forever.

At that point, the band was getting almost as many one night jobs as we could handle. However, it was still not enough to be considered a full-time living. About that time we started considering playing in night clubs. My dad had recently signed with a local booking agency to work part-time as an agent. He typically visited some of the clubs by 9:00PM, and then went to work at his full-time job by midnight, since he was on the night shift. I felt like once the band was working full-time in night clubs I could finally ask Judi to marry me. Many of the night club musicians I knew had been working for over twenty years as full-time musicians. I felt that once I had achieved that level of job security, everything would be fine.

Only two of the members of the band were over twenty-one. We wanted to gain full-time employment working and performing in night clubs. In the early 1970s, there were over three hundred night clubs in the Tampa Bay, Clearwater, and St. Petersburg area that hosted full-time live music. They ranged from piano bars to clubs that would have multiple bands. A musician could literally make a full-time living performing. The difficult part was breaking into the local circuit. Nobody would give us a chance.

### Entering the World of Night Clubs

On his way home one day, my dad stopped at the largest, most elite hotel in Tampa. He talked with the hotel's general manger about booking my band. On that particular morning, the manager had just gotten off the phone with one of the local booking agencies. The manger was very tired from being mistreated so many times by such agencies, that he finally had enough. When my dad walked into his office the manger was ready to try something different. After talking to my dad for a few minutes, the manger wanted to know if my band was a brand new act, with no previous track record playing night clubs and not carrying any negative "baggage." After talking for a few more minutes the manager signed an exclusive contract with my dad to have my band perform as the house band. We were given a six month contract. When my dad got home and told us, we were all ecstatic! He had just gotten my band into one of the most exclusive night clubs in Tampa. Some musical acts worked in the area for twenty years and still had not gotten the chance to play at the Hilton.

After we started playing at the Hilton, I proposed to Judi and she accepted. We were married on the following July 4th, Independence Day!

For the next three years, my band played in some of the most elite night clubs in Tampa. What a ride! I went back to school part-time at the local university. During that time the band went through several configurations and members. Judi sang in some of them.

My night club experience was probably the hardest on my heart. We normally played from 9:00PM until 2:00AM, six nights a week with Sunday off. Even for somebody who is healthy, that type of a schedule is very hard on the body. For me, I lived in a perpetual state of exhaustion, yet I continued to do that for ten years!

Of course, the only consistent thing in life is that change is inevitable. In 1975, the bottom fell out of the entertainment industry. A recession hit Tampa really hard. It also hit the hotels and night clubs. Most of the clubs were not able to continue paying union salaries. All of the members of my band were full-time union musicians. To stay working in the Tampa Bay area, we would have had to work for about half as much as we had previously. Because we were union musicians, it was not legal for us to do so. Because of that fact, we started considering going on the road to make a living.

# Chapter 8
# Life on the Road

At that time, our drummer, whose home was in Connecticut, knew of a big management agency based in her hometown. So, after much discussion about going on the road, we recorded a demo tape and had pictures taken for her to take to the agency while she was there visiting her parents. Within a few weeks the president of the management agency called me. We talked for a while and he decided to take a chance with us and booked us for an audition job at a Holiday Inn in Blacksburg, Virginia. Before we knew it, we were on the road. The job in Virginia turned out to be the perfect first touring job for us. We were a smash hit! Even though we were only a four-piece group, we all played multiple instruments and sang, which really appealed to the audiences. We played all styles. After the audition job, we were booked solid for over two years in advance.

While on the road touring, I performed with two of my own groups and then eventually worked with The Jim Wilkes Road Show for a year. Between the different bands we played for a series of hotel chains including The Ramada Inn, The Holiday Inn, The Scottish Inn, The Red Carpet Inn, and numerous others. We eventually performed in thirty-seven different states. We even toured all the way to southern Iowa playing in an establishment called "The Pizzazzatorium." It had several different night clubs and even a movie theatre within.

## Heart Dancing to the Music

While touring, I had countless "maybes" where my heart would go into arrhythmia for a few minutes at a time and then convert back into normal rhythm. This happened literally anytime, even when I was on the stage. Somehow I could always keep going. I would just stop what I was doing or lean against a wall for a few minutes until I felt better and then resume what I was doing. I would feel SO fatigued that some days I wished that God would just come get me and let me rest!

## Playing a Country Tune

While I was working playing flute and saxophone for The Jim Wilkes Road Show (and Judi was the vocalist), I heard that Razzy Bailey might need a bass player. Razzy was a country artist based in Macon, Georgia. After much discussion, we decided we needed a change so I auditioned for him. The audition meant that I had to drive up to Georgia from Tampa where we were still based, and actually start working for him. It was an on-the-job audition. After a couple nights of playing bass guitar it was decided that I, indeed, was good enough to work for him. So my newest journey began. At that time, Razzy was performing around the Georgia, Alabama, Tennessee, and North and South Carolina area. He was in between record label contracts and was focusing on primarily working at two major night clubs that featured country music. They were both located in Macon, Georgia. These were big night clubs capable of hosting hundreds of people each night. My salary was based on working six nights a week. At the time it was excellent pay.

At first it was exciting because of the clientele that came in and the other musicians I was exposed to by playing in Razzy's group. For example, while we were performing at times, literally a "who's who" of record label artists would show up and jam with us. During the two years I worked for him I backed up most of the major country recording stars at the time, and even got to perform alongside some of the biggest names in the music business. For instance, I got to work alongside Johnnie Lee Johnson (Allman Brothers Band), Chuck Level (The Rolling Stones), the group Alabama, as well as members of the Marshal Tucker Band, the Charlie Daniels Band and many others. Other artists would often just "drop by" and be seen sitting in the night club. Some of them included Greg Allman and Cher, as well as others. At that time, Macon, Georgia was the recording mecca for major Southern rock artists because Capricorn Records was located there.

In the spring of 1978, I realized that while I was working for Razzy I was just a puppet. I was not in control of my life. I had gotten to know many of the other full-time working musicians in the Middle Georgia area. Most of them were in their mid- to late-forties, divorced, and smoking and drinking a lot. Some of them even took drugs. They were miserable. I did not want to end up like them. One of them even told me to get out while I could! I wanted more out of my life.

There was a much darker side to the music industry that most people don't see. Drugs and sex were a major component of the environment. Many times I was the *only* musician who went home to his own wife and did not take any drugs nor alcohol. I had numerous opportunities for both sex and drugs. There were many times I was the only one NOT partaking in those activities. I really felt like a loner. (I was mistakenly under the illusion that the reason for playing in night clubs was to foster and build a career in music, not for sex and drugs!) I began to realize that I needed to get out of it before it was too late, and go back to school.

### Heart Troubles During This Time

While I was working for Razzy, I had my first full-blown cardiac event where my heart actually stopped beating. I had gone to the dentist to have my wisdom teeth removed. I was in my twenties. The dentist convinced me that he could give me local anesthesia and that I would be fine. What was unknown to both the dentist and me was that my heart was going to do something very new. Right in the middle of the surgery my heart stopped. My wife later told me that she was relaxing in the waiting area when she heard the nurse scream that I was not breathing. Both the nurse and the dentist began slapping and shaking me. My wife said that she could hear them slapping me! Apparently after a minute or so my heart started up again and I regained consciousness. While my heart had stopped I remember floating near the ceiling of the room looking down at the dentist and nurse slapping and shaking me. I remember how peaceful everything was.

This happened several more times during that period in my life (in my middle to late twenties). It happened at home and when I was hospitalized in intensive care. Each time my heart would completely stop and then start again after a period of time. Both of my brothers had a similar episode only once in their lives. My middle brother was in college sitting at his desk and just collapsed on the floor with no pulse. After a minute or so his heart restarted and he regained consciousness. My youngest brother was home watching a football game. When he got up to go to the kitchen, his heart stopped and he collapsed to the floor shattering his shoulder as he fell. After a period of time his heart also restarted and he regained consciousness. But he had shattered his shoulder and had to have an artificial shoulder joint put in. It is interesting to note that all three of us had similar heart problems around the same time in our lives (in our twenties). It is assumed there is a genetic link in the family for this type of problem.

# SECTION III
# Settling into Adulthood

# Chapter 9
# Going Back to School

About that time something inside of me was telling me to go back to school. In fact, the voice was practically *screaming* at me to go back to school! In Macon, Georgia, there was a small private liberal arts university named Mercer University. (Since then, it has grown to be one of the largest private schools in the Southeast.) During the day, I usually hung out in the music department at Mercer, even before I started taking classes. I grew to know several of the music professors very well.

### *Scholarships from Heaven*

One afternoon while I was hanging out in the music department, the band director saw me and asked to speak with me. He asked me if I was going to continue to work in night clubs and work for Razzy the rest of my life, or was I going to take charge of my life and go back to school? I was twenty-eight and I had been a full-time musician for almost ten years. Well that little voice inside of me was screaming at me then! I finally listened to it. After I auditioned, the music department awarded me the most fantastic combination music/academic scholarship I could ever receive. (Remember, my high school AND collegiate grades were both a C minus average, and no better.)

When they told me about the academic scholarship, I reminded them of my very weak scholastic record. I could not believe that they would award anybody scholarship money with an academic record like mine. Their response absolutely astounded me. They told me that they had the ultimate faith that I would not let them down and that I would attain the high level of academic achievement that would be required of me. I almost cried right there. Here was a major university showing so much faith in me when I did not have that in myself.

My education was almost totally paid for between the two scholarships. I only needed money to live on while I was in school. The arrangement was that in return for the scholarships I received, they could showcase me to help advertise their music department by my performing alongside their music faculty and other music department sponsored events.

I gave Razzy my two week notice and never looked back. He signed with RCA records and I went back to school. While writing this, I realized that going back to school was another turning point in my life. The professors at Mercer University were another group of angels sent to help me at that point of my life.

## *Performance Opportunities of a Lifetime*

While I attended Mercer University, I performed alongside most of the music faculty, guest artists, and numerous other music professionals. There were many (and sometimes humorous) events for me musically while I was attending Mercer and beyond graduation. When I went back to college, I also joined the local musicians' union. Because I could play flute, clarinet, saxophone, and electric bass at the professional level, I was soon raised to the position of "first call." (That means when a musical organization calls the musicians' union needing professional players, I was first on the list to be called for my instruments.)

During my freshman year, I got a call from someone needing a bass player when their group came through Macon on their Southeast tour for the next month. When the caller identified who he was, at first I did not believe him and told him so. I figured it was someone I knew in town who was joking with me. He identified himself as the music director for The Lettermen. (They were a three man vocal group that had a series of number one hits back in the 1970s through 1980s.) I still did not believe him and told him so a second time. He assured me that he was who he said he was and told me that he got my name from the local musicians' union and that I was given an "A" rating as a player. Still not believing who he was, I decided to hear him out. He explained that their bass player had a conflict on that date and they needed a bass player for the Macon concert. So I agreed to the job, and we hung up. Still not believing who he said he was, I called people I knew in an effort to determine who was joking with me.

After two weeks of trying to find the guilty culprit, I gave up and figured that I would have to show up for the job to see if it was for real. So, on the day of the supposed Lettermen concert, I loaded my equipment and headed to the Grand Opera House in Macon. Once I arrived, I looked on the marquee and it had The Lettermen concert listed for that night. That's when I started thinking that maybe this was the "real deal" after all. *Then* I started to get nervous. After all, these guys were national recording artists with many gold records to their credit. I found the side door to the opera house stage and carried my equipment inside. When I reached the stage, I saw them. It really was The Lettermen! I just about had a heart attack. Until then, I thought this whole thing was a joke being played on me. But this was for real!

As I pulled my dolly over with my bass amp, one of The Lettermen walked over and started talking with me. In turn, each of them introduced themselves to me. Then they introduced me to the music director and the other musicians they brought along. When the music director introduced himself to me, I realized that he WAS the man I spoke with over the phone. This was as real as it could get! I immediately apologized for not believing him when we talked previously. He told me that it happens a lot and not to worry about it.

We got down to work and ran through some of the music for the evening concert. Later that night we presented the concert. It was a real pleasure working with musicians of their caliber. Most of the instrumentalists were full-time musicians based out of Los Angeles. The Lettermen and the band musicians all treated me very well. They were all first rate gentlemen!

### *Join the Circus?*

Probably the most difficult music job for me was when I was called to play bass for the Barnum & Bailey Circus. I know, I know. Most people think that a circus band plays nothing but circus marches and such. Well maybe one-hundred years ago they may have, but *that* circus band played major world class arrangements that would have worked well for The Tonight Show Band.

Again, I was not sure if this was the "real deal" until I pulled up to the Macon Coliseum, a big arena that could seat up to 10,000 people. On the marquee I saw the circus being advertised, and realized that this was for real. Then, as I drove around to unload my car I almost ran into several elephants that were being led to the back of the coliseum. As I pulled my bass amp into the building there were seemingly hundreds of people running about very busily preparing for their first performance which was that evening. I found the area where the circus band was to be seated and introduced myself to the director. The band that traveled with the circus had a core group of six musicians. The rest of the band were musicians hired from the local musicians' union. Normally their bass player traveled with them. But in this case he was very ill and in the hospital. So when they came to Macon, they were forced to hire a bass player for the job.

Once I was set up, I started to look at the music book for the night. There was over two and a half hours of music! The worst part was that it was an extreme mixture of all styles. The styles ranged from pop, country, hard core jazz, rock, and disco, to other styles. I was mortified! After all, I *did* play bass, but this job was going to be the most difficult musical commitment I had to that point. All the director did during the rehearsal was start a dozen or so songs with us. After that, he said that was enough and he would see us that night. We did not even go through all of the music. I started to realize that I was going to sight-read over two hours of music in front of 10,000 people! And to make matters worse, my bass amp had a microphone placed in front of it by their sound technician, and it was going to be pumped through their main public address system for the coliseum! I could not hide at all!

As I sat there still stunned, the director walked over to the lead trumpet player that he had just hired, and told him in a matter of fact way, that he could not cut the music and fired him on the spot. To make matters worse the director then started to walk over to me. At that point I figured I was next. He was going to fire me too! As I started to pack up my bass, he asked, "What are you doing?" I told him that I figured he was going to fire me also. He laughed and said that actually he was going to ask if I could play bass for them when they toured through Florida the next week. Still stunned by the whole ordeal, I had to politely decline the offer to go with them. (I was already committed the entire week.) They ended up hiring the principal trumpet player from the Atlanta Symphony to cover the trumpet part for the week. The circus performed an evening show on Wednesday, Thursday and Friday, three shows on Saturday, and two more on Sunday. All the band members treated me wonderfully that whole time. I had a lot of fun performing with them. I was ready to join the circus!

## Other Exciting Performances

At the same coliseum, I played with two different touring shows featuring ice skaters. One was the Holiday on Ice Show and the other was the Ice Capades Show. One of the shows featured Olympic gold medalist Dorothy Hamill and the other show featured Olympic gold medalist Peggy Fleming. For both of those shows, I played flute, clarinet, and tenor saxophone. I actually got to meet both of the Olympic skaters backstage. On the ice they looked larger than life. In reality, they were both small, petite women. The only negative point about those jobs was that the band was positioned right on the floor of the coliseum. We were *literally* on the ice! They put plywood and carpet over the ice for us, but after a three hour performance it still was very cold! We even had to play to a pre-recorded soundtrack that had strings and voices on it. The live instruments mixed with the prerecorded music worked very well for the event. All of the musicians who toured with the shows were Los Angeles full-time musicians. It was very intense, but a lot of fun.

## The Macon Symphony

At about the time I returned to school at Mercer University, the city of Macon was starting up a professional symphony. So naturally, I auditioned. As it turned out the new conductor was also a flutist. Well after a few days I found out, once again, that I did not make the cut. Because of my past, I was devastated. But I kept my head up and concentrated on my academic studies. When I attended their first symphony concert I could not help but cry through the entire event. I really wanted to be a part of that level of music. I did notice that they had only accepted two flutists. Well just a few days after their first concert, I got a call from the conductor. He said that he had hired the two other flutists for the fall concert because they both had some orchestral experience. (I had none at that time.) Then he went on to say I actually had given one of the best auditions, and that he decided that I should be a part of the growing orchestra for the city of Macon. I was truly delighted! I played principal second flute with that orchestra all through my undergraduate degree. I only gave up my position when I moved out of state to attend graduate school.

### Continued Opportunities

While attending Mercer I worked full-time in a local night club band, playing saxophone and flute. We usually performed three weeks in every month. The downside was that the hours were from 9:00PM until about 2:00AM, so I was only getting four to five hours of sleep at night. By the middle of my first semester of study I discovered a lounge chair that was hidden from view in the back of the library. It became my unofficial place of refuge. I went there practically every day to rest up to an hour.

The band auditioned and won a spot to compete in the "Search 2" contest. It was hosted by Ed McMahon, who worked with Johnny Carson on The Tonight Show. We came in second in the Southeastern Division! With that, we went to Atlanta where we taped a program for Georgia Public Television. The show was aired later that year.

Even after graduating from Mercer University, I continued working as a freelance musician. I performed with several other major artists such as The Four Tops, The Temptations, Blackstone the Magician, and many others. As I backed up the national level artists I was asked more than once if I wanted to work for them. I had several opportunities to tour and record on the national stage with some of the biggest recording stars of the time. For some reason I always politely declined. I didn't know at the time but there was a different direction where God was guiding me.

### Health Issues While in School

While I was in undergraduate school at Mercer University, I was in intensive care in the cardiac unit in total arrhythmia countless times. It was so bad that I was on a first name basis with most of the medical staff at several hospitals in the Middle Georgia area! Back in the 1980s to 1990s, all they could do for me was keep adding medication to control the arrhythmia, which meant I felt totally horrible all the time. At one point, I was on three different heart medications at the same time.

Anytime I went into full arrhythmia I could not walk, sit up, nor function at all. All I could do was lie in bed. My heart rate would race over 200 beats per minute while in atrial fibrillation. Within a few hours fluid would start building up in my chest. It was very dangerous. My wife would either take me to the hospital or call the ambulance. Once in the hospital I would be given massive amounts of heart drugs in an attempt to put the heart back into normal rhythm. It could take days or even weeks for the heart to stabilize and go back into normal rhythm. It seemed like every few months I would be back in the hospital going through the same procedure. This continued while I was attending Mercer University, working on my undergraduate degree.

By my senior year in college I had collapsed twice from exhaustion from the combination of heart medications, workload from college, and lack of sleep from performing at night. So when I started on my last semester as a senior, I gave my two weeks' notice to the band and prayed that I could make enough money from my freelancing and teaching lessons to survive. Somehow we survived financially through graduation.

# Chapter 10
# Working as a Band Director

After graduating from Mercer University, I started to work as a band director that next fall. On the side, I joined another band that played predominantly in country clubs and private parties on weekends. Everybody else in the band had been together since they were young. The band had a huge following! I played mainly saxophone and flute with them. We played hits from the Sixties, Seventies, and Eighties. I stayed with them until I went back to school to start on my doctoral degree in 1992.

Because I was fresh out of college with no band directing experience, the only job I could get was at a rural county middle/high school over forty-five miles away. They had gone through a number of band directors in recent years. Because of severe discipline problems with students at both the middle and high schools, several band directors even resigned in the middle of the school year. Although the school was located in a rural area of Georgia, there were a lot of problems with drugs and alcohol. I was assigned to teach four periods of middle school band and two periods of high school band every day. It was a very rough situation and it was obvious that there was no discipline nor structure in the band program.

Even when I interviewed for the job, I saw several students using four-letter words while they were backtalking the teacher. As I was observing the class, one of the students was describing, in sexual terms, what he would like to do to the band director who was a lady. The high school principal was right there beside me and did not say a word! The high school band had never marched, never had any uniforms, and the students had very low opinion of themselves. Most of the equipment was badly damaged and very old. It was obvious that I would have my work cut out for me.

I had conflict with practically every student from the beginning. The students in the band had no discipline whatsoever. They were like wild animals. The middle school administration supported me one hundred percent on anything I needed to do to turn the program around. My problem was with the high school principal. He did not want me to be so strict with everything because he was afraid I might offend or upset someone.

To make matters worse, I had doubts about myself being able to successfully do what was needed to turn the band program around because of my past. I had to reach very deep inside to draw the strength I would need to turn that band program around. After praying for help I thought I was ready.

I was hired to start and build a marching band which meant that we needed to prepare several shows for the football games and marching competitions. So after talking to the superintendent, I called for a band camp two weeks before school started to help prepare the high school band for their first halftime show. They had never been required to attend a summer camp before.

### *Band Camp Nightmare*

On the first day of band camp over ninety high school students showed up and assembled in the band room. I tried to get their attention so that I could go over the day's itinerary but no one would pay attention to me. Some of them were busy talking. Some were playing their instruments. Others were running around the band room. After five minutes of trying to get their attention I was ready to quit! I had no other adult to help me. There was no other teacher around. I was the only adult in the band room. I started praying to God to help me! This was too much for me. As I was just about to give up and leave, a voice inside of me said that He would help me through this. The voice calmed me down. A short while later I no longer felt helpless nor afraid. That was when I realized I was not alone! God was there to help me.

Once I finished praying I realized that the situation had not changed. I needed to find a way to get their attention. So for a few moments I pondered what to do. I realized that I needed to do something very strong that would really get their attention and make a statement about myself. I picked up my conductor's podium and threw it across the room. There were a lot of shrieks from the band students. The band room immediately got very quiet. As I looked around the band room I realized that I finally had their attention. So I began to speak, and that is how I started band camp.

Although totally opposite from my normal character, I had to run the band program like it was boot camp. I had to be extremely strict. What I soon discovered was that ninety-five percent of the students were typical wonderful young adults. The other five percent were like the "hoods" I had to deal with while growing up. They would cheat, steal, lie, fleece other students, drink alcohol, and take and sell drugs while in school. They were so evil that I even had to be careful around them for my own safety.

By the end of band camp I had tried to kick most of the "hoods" out of the band program. They would not obey me, and they were very disrespectful of me and everyone else, including their fellow students. They talked back to me and even threatened me. When I was done for the day, they would hang around the band room and even my car. More than once, if I disciplined them for something, I would find new scratch marks (made by their car keys) on my new car afterwards. Even the other students were afraid of them. Unfortunately the high school principal would not allow me to remove them from the program nor fail them. He was afraid of what they might do to the school if they got mad. Most of them were quite a bit older than the rest of the students even though they were still in high school. The battle with me wanting to remove the "hoods" from my band program continued throughout the school year.

With the backing of the superintendent and middle school principal I slowly started to turn the program around. By the end of the two week band camp the high school band was ready for their first football game. As I said earlier most of the students were great to work with. Once I set the standards, most of the students were fine and cooperated.


### *Health Issues Again*

Of course with all of my health issues, it's no surprise that a problem surfaced. On the last day of band camp I came down with double pneumonia. I was hospitalized in intensive care for almost a week. Unfortunately, I was still in the hospital on the day of the first football game when the band was supposed to perform. What I did not know was that some of the good students in the band had planned a surprise for me. A group of them had gone to the middle school principal and superintendent and asked if they could still perform in the halftime show even though I was in the hospital.

The superintendent agreed on the condition that the middle school principal would act as the sponsor and watch the band at the game. Later that evening the nurse picked up the phone near my bed (I was still on heavy medications and hooked up with tubes and wires) and handed it to me. On the phone I could hear my school band performing their halftime show live via the phone lines. I listened and cried at the same time. I had gone from an abused child to being a professional music educator.

### Student/Principal Troubles

As the year moved on the band really started to progress. With the exception of the "hoods," all of the band students were enjoying the program. They were always at school early and stayed late to help me out with anything that needed to be done. The booster club got so excited that they purchased brand new uniforms for the band. We even started a flag line! Everything was going well for me except for the "hoods." They took advantage of any opportunity they had to interfere with me trying to develop the band. I found my brand new drum heads smashed in and snare drum and bass drum sticks were stolen. They did whatever they could to sabotage the band program. Every time I caught one of them breaking or stealing something I reported it to the high school principal but no disciplinary action took place. These "hoods" knew that they would not be punished. They thought that they could get away with anything, and seemingly they were right. This type of torment went on for several months.

The final straw for me occurred when I had another disagreement with the high school principal over students at a basketball pep band event. When the drummers arrived (all in one car) it was obvious they were extremely intoxicated. As they walked into the band room I immediately told them to turn around and go home and sleep it off. Well, instead of going home they got extremely belligerent and started threatening me. Then they started picking up chairs, music stands, and even musical instruments and started throwing them around the band room. I tried to get them to stop but they grabbed me and started pushing me around and threatening me some more. I instantly realized that this was out of my control so I ran into my office and called the police. Once they realized I had called the police they ran out of the band room and took off in their car. I then called the high school principal and informed him what had taken place. He told me not to do nor saying anything more. Then he said he wanted to see me in his office first thing in the morning.

The next morning I arrived at his office before classes started. He went on to say that he had to *undo* all the damage *I* had caused the night before with the students. He also told me that he wished that I had not called the police. He said that I only made it much worse! He said that I really created some waves in the community over what I did to those poor students. He then told me, "You know, boys will be boys, and they don't mean any harm." I then said, "What? They were destroying the band room and also threatening *me* with harm!" He went on to say that it could not have been all that bad and that I should just forget about it. I told him that I had had enough of those particular students and that I wanted them out of the band program. Then he informed me that he would not allow me to take them out of the band program. He told me to just stick them in the back of the band room for a few days and then put them back in the band. That was the moment I realized that he was more afraid of the "hoods" than I was. Here he was, the high school principal, and he didn't have the inner strength to do his job properly. It's no wonder the music program had been in such a shambles. The high school principal was afraid to properly discipline the students. There was no support from the high school administration. I was stronger than he was in dealing with the "hoods"! That was when I decided (in mid-year) that I would not be working at that school the next year.

## *Déjà vu*

While working there, aside from all the turmoil with some of the band members, I witnessed bullying among students like I had endured when I was in school. Part of my duties as a teacher was to monitor the cafeteria during lunch. I had only been there a month when I caught a student trying to fleece another student of his lunch food. The "hood" calmly walked over to another student and helped himself to some food off the other student's plate. When I saw the victim start to cry, I knew immediately what had happened. I was determined not to let another student go through the same torment I had endured while growing up. So I walked over to confirm what I had just witnessed. After talking to the victim, I went right over to the student who had taken the food, and hauled him off to the office. The student was suspended from school for several days by the middle school principal. He told me that it was a fairly common occurrence and he appreciated my attentiveness to the matter. I told him that while on my watch, I would never allow that to happen again!

## *Success in Spite of it All*

By June I had completed my first year there as the band director. I had developed a high school marching and concert band that the community was very proud of. I felt like I had done my best despite what I had to endure. When I turned in my resignation the middle school principal pleaded with me to stay. The superintendent begged me to stay and even offered to double my supplemental salary. The high school principal did not say a word to me. To this day some of the "good" students from that band program STILL stay in touch with me. What was really amazing to me was the fact that I did not go into full arrhythmia that year, despite what I had to endure. God was with me.

## *Coping with the Heart*

After starting to work as a band director that year, there were many times my wife had to help drag me out of bed to go to work. My heart medications had been increased and were making it hard to function. It seemed so unfair to me. I was just starting my career as a band director and I had to live with this heart problem. The arrhythmia could happen anytime. Back then, it was common for me to feel out of sorts and very tired for several hours as my heart was going in and out of arrhythmia, before finally going into sustained atrial fibrillation. It could happen day or night. It could happen from a sudden shock, such as a loud noise going off near me, or a dog scaring me (which actually happened). I would suddenly go from a normal heart rhythm into total arrhythmia. I started on my heart medications in my twenties and have been on them through my entire adult life.

# Chapter 11
# Achieving Graduate Degrees
# Despite Heart Troubles

During the years I worked on my master's degree (in the mid-1980s), my heart went in and out of arrhythmia every day. I was spared full-blown atrial fibrillation for those years, although I had the same chronic fatigue problem that I did earlier. It was due to the combination of intermittent heart arrhythmia and the strong medications.

When I started the doctoral degree I was surprised that my heart did not get any worse than it was. I worked on my degree from 1992 through 1998 and my heart acted up almost daily with intermittent arrhythmia. Then at times, it would be "quiet" for a few days, and then repeat the cycle once again.

The worst event during that time was when I was getting ready for a major concert with the woodwind quintet that I was a member of at the University of Georgia in Athens. We were all doctoral students. We were getting ready to perform at a professional woodwind quintet concert competition. There were woodwind quintets from leading universities around the country. I was warming up and noticed that my heart was going in and out of arrhythmia. I wasn't too worried because this had been the usual pattern for years. Then suddenly it went into full-blown atrial fibrillation. I was stunned! All I could think about was how I was going to perform if I was lying on the floor! I didn't know what to do. Nobody in the group had the slightest inclination that I had a heart problem. I usually don't tell people because I never want anyone to feel sorry for me nor pity me. At that time the rest of the quintet came over to see why I was sitting on the floor instead of warming up. As best as I could talk between gasping for oxygen, I told them about my heart arrhythmia situation. I really thought they would all be upset with me for possibly causing our performance to be cancelled. But to my astonishment they were all genuinely very concerned. I instructed them to help me get up and slowly walk me around while I tried some breathing tricks I learned that occasionally helped. I prayed very hard as they were walking me around the room. After about five minutes my heart slipped back into normal rhythm enough that I was able to play the concert.

The largest problem I had with my heart while I was working on my doctoral degree was the intermittent arrhythmia. Many times it would act up continuously for several hours and even sometimes several days while I was attending classes, giving a major performance, or participating in music juries. More than once I felt so bad I wanted to quit. Many times I could not do my best in a music jury or performance because of the way I felt. I was lucky to be able to stand up, let alone perform at my best! Because of my class and work schedule and practicing flute eight to ten hours each day, I was forced to get up at 5:00AM but usually did not get into bed before midnight. When factoring in the double heart medications I was taking AND the extreme tiredness and weakness from the heart arrhythmia, it is a wonder I completed my degree.

# Chapter 12
# Teaching College with Arrhythmia

I graduated with my doctoral degree from The University of Georgia in 1998. In 1999, I was hired for my first full-time college position as the director of bands at a small college in Nebraska, Peru State College. I loved the college but there was little else in the area for me or my family, so I soon started looking for a school in a larger community. During that time my heart was starting to act up even more, sometimes several times a day. The increased intermittent heart arrhythmia continued until I got the job at Buena Vista University (BVU) in Iowa in 2001.

Because of the expense, we moved ourselves. This meant we had to do the loading and unloading of the moving truck. We *did* have the help of our two sons and some of their friends. The very next day after we moved into our new home, my heart went into full atrial fibrillation. My wife drove me to the hospital. This time my heart would not reset itself. After many days in the hospital they sent me home where I was to remain until the medications triggered my heart to go back into normal rhythm. It took a month. Luckily for me, it was the summer and I had not yet started my new job at the university. That was the worst experience I had faced to that point with my heart problem. By then I was on three medications to try to control the arrhythmia.

In late August, I was attending meetings for faculty members during the week before school started, when it happened again. The day before the students were scheduled to report to the campus I went into full-blown atrial fibrillation again. To make matters even worse, I was supposed to perform for the opening convocation ceremonies for the freshman class the next day. Well, I was taken to intensive care and my poor wife had to call the school and tell them the bad news. Fortunately, the school organist was able to cover for me by providing music for the event. The doctors decided to increase the medications I was already on and within a week my heart went back into normal rhythm. The increased heart medicines were devastating to me. I looked and felt horrible! It got so bad my poor wife would have to literally drag me out of bed to help me get up to go to work. All my co-workers told me that I looked and acted like a zombie! I wanted to die! I could not understand why I had to live like this.

### *Heart Dancing to the Music*

My fall jazz band concert was scheduled during my first semester working at BVU. Well, you guessed it! My heart was in and out of arrhythmia all the day of the program. Right before the concert began (literally two to three minutes beforehand), my heart went into full atrial fibrillation again. I was backstage, ready to walk on and start the concert, and I was in arrhythmia. There were over 350 people in the audience ready to hear the university jazz ensemble perform. I panicked! Only a very select few people on the campus knew anything about my heart problems. I did not know what to do. Then I came up with an idea. I stumbled on stage, practically dragging my feet, and snuggled up to the side of the piano for support and directed the concert leaning on the piano. Fortunately for me, as a jazz director you do not have to conduct all the music as you would an orchestra. The jazz director just starts the songs and gives cues during the music. Through the entire concert I was practically in and out of consciousness the whole time. Immediately after the concert my wife came up to the stage and helped me off and then drove me to the hospital where, once again, I was placed in intensive care in the cardiology unit.

The next day the president of the university showed up at the hospital wanting to know what happened to me. He was at the concert the night before. I had done pretty well not letting anyone know about my condition until then. Fortunately the college has stood behind me all the way with my health issues.

### Saved by the Nurses?

At the hospital I went through the usual treatment. They gave me more and more drugs but the heart would not go back into normal rhythm. One of the local doctors suggested that he could perform a cardioversion on me, which is where they subject the heart to an electric shock to convert it back into a normal rhythm. I asked him how serious it would be and he stated that it was not a big deal at all. (Note that this was in a small town hospital.) So we set it up for later that evening. As soon as he left the room several nurses came running in to talk to me. They looked very serious. They STRONGLY suggested that I should not let the doctor perform the cardioversion on me. When I asked them why, they stated that the hospital was not set up for such a serious life-threatening procedure. They even offered to arrange ambulance transportation and do all the paperwork to have me taken to a major heart center in the next city seventy miles away. What could I say to *that*?! I agreed and was transported to a major heart facility in Sioux City (Iowa) where the cardioversion procedure took place.

### *Resurrected?*

Here's yet another heart episode that also happened within my first year of teaching at BVU. Since I was unconscious part of this time, I cannot recount exactly what happened, so my wife filled in the blanks...

I encountered another atrial fibrillation episode and went to the local hospital to have it checked out. They monitored me and attempted to have the heart return to a normal rhythm through medications, but they were unsuccessful. Probably because of insurance regulations, they sent me home. However when leaving the hospital, the nurse looked squarely at my wife and said, "If ANYTHING happens, anything at all — don't hesitate to call 911." That statement had a profound impact on Judi, as the seriousness of the situation struck her hard.

Well, something *did* happen. In the middle of the night, Judi woke up feeling the house shake. We don't know if God was "shaking" the house to wake her up, or if she felt vibrations from when I fell. However, she was in a sound sleep, so we're inclined to think the first option was the case. She woke up from feeling the house shaking and realized I wasn't in the bed. She immediately got up and looked around for me. Apparently, I had gotten up to use the bathroom, then passed out while on the way back to the bedroom. She saw that I was unconscious and immediately called 911. Paramedics were sent to the house.

It didn't take long for them to arrive, as we were in a very small town at the time. They checked me out and couldn't find a pulse, nor could they detect a heartbeat. They looked at each other very briefly, as if they were indicating I had died. However, I was still barely breathing. So, one of them directed another paramedic to put the oxygen on my face, which he did. Everyone just stood there and watched me as I laid there unconscious. Then, after a brief time, I regained consciousness. With that, they wrapped me up, put me in a transport chair to move me down the stairs, and loaded me into the ambulance. Back to the hospital I went and spent several days, once again, in intensive care.

One of the paramedics knew the pastor of the church we were attending at the time. He told him the story and they all interpreted the event as if I had died and was brought back to life by a divine force. They did not administer cardiopulmonary resuscitation. I came to on my own. I can't say if it was divine intervention or not, but for quite some time thereafter, the pastor made continual comments about my having been "resurrected."

# Chapter 13
# New Surgical Procedure for My Heart

While in the cardiology unit at the hospital in Sioux City after *yet another* atrial fibrillation episode, the doctors were able to stabilize and convert my heart back to normal rhythm within a few days. While I was being evaluated by the cardiologist, he told me about a new procedure that might correct my heart problem. It was called ablation surgery. He told me that they could schedule the heart ablation for me and that it would take place at a leading heart center in Omaha (Nebraska). After I was released from the Sioux City hospital I scheduled the ablation procedure to be done in Omaha.

### My First Ablation Surgery...Temporary Success

Immediately after the ablation surgery I felt a million times better, even though I was still on the heart drugs! In fact, the procedure was so successful that I did not have any heart rhythm problems for over five years. During that time, my wife and I purchased a one-hundred-year-old, 10,000 square foot commercial building in a town near Buena Vista University, where I was still working. We gutted all three floors and built a 2,300 square foot apartment on the top floor, a commercial bakery/bistro/kitchen supply store on the main floor and a 1,700 square foot recording studio in the basement. Maybe God had finally listened to my prayers! I felt like Superman!!

About five years after my first ablation surgery the intermittent heart arrhythmia problems slowly started to return. Then one day I was outside walking with my wife and bingo — I went into full atrial fibrillation again. At the hospital, after failing to convert my heart back into normal rhythm with increased medication, the doctor cardioverted my heart and the heart rhythm was stabilized.

### *More Ablation Surgeries*

Then I had my second ablation surgery. It worked for a few months until I was back in intensive care again with atrial fibrillation. After I was cardioverted again, they scheduled yet a third ablation surgery for me. It was after the third ablation surgery that the doctor felt confident enough that he began to slowly wean me off all heart medications. Within one month after I was off the medications, I went into full-blown atrial fibrillation *again*.

It was during that time that I gave up hope. I didn't know what to do. The doctors began talking to me about living in permanent arrhythmia. The only other thing they could do was give me enough heart medications to possibly slow down the frequency of the occurrences. The problem for me was that more medications meant I could not work nor function normally. I had been on that level of heart medications before and I knew what it would be like. I would be unable to do anything but sit in a chair and stare at the television all day. I was scared to death of this possibility. I had reached the point where I did not want to live any more. I had finally given up. I had been a fighter dealing with my health problems all of my life. I was finally too tired to continue anymore. After my wife left the hospital that evening I began to cry. I could not stop crying. I was terrified of what would come next in my life. I always felt that, to some extent, I was in control of my life. At that moment I felt very helpless and alone. I cried out to God for help!

I always had this confusion with God over my music. I knew that He gave me the gift of music. From day one, I seemed to know that music would be my life. But why did I have to suffer so much with my health, particularly when it conflicted with my using God's gift? There was a time when we were living in Georgia when my heart was acting up so much that for over ten years I hardly used my musical talents at all. I was afraid that I might go into arrhythmia during a performance. I was the unhappiest person in the world during that time.

Previously, every time I went back in the hospital in arrhythmia I was always thinking about what I was going to do when I was released. I was usually fairly upbeat. But as I lay in the hospital bed that particular evening, for some reason, I knew it was different this time. I was too tired to fight the fight anymore. I had been fighting this battle my entire life and I had had enough. I begged God to take me home. At that moment, I looked up and told God that I could not deal with it anymore. As I was looking up and talking to God, gradually a calmness came over me. It was as if a great weight had been lifted off of my shoulders. I continued to talk to God the rest of the evening. That was when I began to realize that I was not in control of my life — God was.

After a few days in arrhythmia I saw my personal cardiologist and he did a cardioversion (once again) on me to convert my heart back to normal rhythm. During the last ten years (from the time I'm writing this) I have been cardioverted many times. After that episode with my heart arrhythmia, the doctor told me there was nothing more he could do for me. He said that I may have to live in permanent arrhythmia.

As of this writing I have gone into two more full-blown atrial fibrillation episodes since my last ablation surgery. Each time the heart has gone back into normal rhythm within a few hours which indicates to me that the three ablation surgeries have helped, but did not completely correct the problem. I was uplifted somewhat at a recent visit with my cardiologist. He said there was a new procedure that he could possibly try on me the next time it happens. At least there is some hope.

# Chapter 14
# ADHD

I had another issue with my health that I was not aware of until after I became an adult. I had grown up with ADD (attention deficit disorder), or more recently it would be referred to as ADHD-I (attention deficit hyperactive disorder, predominantly inattentive type). I did not realize I had all the classic symptoms of ADHD while growing up until recently. My younger son was diagnosed with it after he graduated from high school. Apparently, ADD/ADHD tends to run in families. As I looked back on my life, I realized that I had symptoms similar to those of my son while I was growing up. (Of course, back when I was growing up the doctors knew little of ADD or ADHD.) Even though it appeared on the outside that my brain was not functioning, on the inside my brain was racing a mile a minute, sometimes reaching out and trying to think of several different things at once. I could not sit still, nor focus in class. If I tried to study, after a few minutes my mind was ready to move on to something else. I couldn't sleep at night because my brain was so active. I was extremely hyper on the inside.

To this day, my brain is moving so fast that when I type, I leave out words because my brain has already finished the sentence before my hands could type all the words. Even when I talk I tend to leave out words for the same reason. It is not unusual for me to practice my flute to a metronome while watching a video and reading the morning news on my computer ALL AT THE SAME TIME.

Typical symptoms of ADHD may include difficulty paying attention to details and making careless mistakes, easily getting distracted, inability to complete tasks, or constantly shifting from one uncompleted activity to another. The predominant problems of mine were easily getting distracted and procrastination. Other problems associated with ADHD may include disorganized work habits and forgetfulness in daily activities. That was and still is to some degree, me.

Children with ADHD need structure and routine. They should be helped to make schedules, and assignments should be divided into smaller tasks to be performed one at a time. I have lived by this method for over thirty years. If I don't set up a very structured routine for myself, whether at work or home, I get nothing accomplished. I still tend to procrastinate a lot if I am not structured.

Medical research has shown that children who were abused are much more prone to developing ADHD. The more severe the abuse, the more intense the condition. Abused children also seem to have a higher rate of autism. For some people, taking stimulants, the standard medication for ADHD, does not work. Doctors have found that certain types of heart arrhythmia medication can actually help some people with ADHD. Beta blockers seem to calm ADHD patients where they can focus and concentrate more clearly. In my case, because of my severe heart arrhythmia, doctors started me on heart medication in my middle twenties. That was when I went back to school and found that I was able to focus on my academics. Before I started the heart medication, my high school and collegiate grade average was always a C. I had serious trouble focusing on my school work and was prone to dropping classes in lieu of failing them. Once I was on the medications, my grade average went through the ceiling (bachelor-3.45, master-3.65, and doctorate-3.75)!

# SECTION IV

## Rebuilding My Life

*(Finding God's Purpose)*

# Chapter 15
# The Shadow Within

Throughout my career as an educator I have been around hundreds, if not thousands of students who were abused in some way. To me, they are very easy to spot and I can recognize them anywhere. When I am walking down a hallway, when I am lecturing in a class, and even when I am eating in the cafeteria, I recognize the physically or emotionally abused child. They walk alone in the hallway always looking down, making sure not to make eye contact. They always walk in a hurry with their shoulders slumped, looking back behind them. When in a class they are always sitting alone. It is almost like everyone knows not to go near that child. Even at lunch they are always alone, again, not making eye contact with anyone. Even the way they dress is different from the rest. They do not want to stick out and be recognized. This is what I was left with when I completed high school. I am one of them. I was an abused child.

A study published in the journal *Pediatrics* showed increased negative long-term health effects in the victims of bullying. After the data was collected the effects due to bullying were clear. The victim's mental health state was directly related to the severity and longevity of the bullying. For many children who suffer abuse on a regular basis, it becomes the only life they know. They may even begin to expect it, thinking the abuse is what they deserve. They may come to believe that it is "normal" treatment (Mahfood 2014).

### Post-Traumatic Stress Disorder (PTSD)

A group of Harvard University researchers, led by Dr. Martin Teicher, conducted a study to examine the effects of abuse in children. They discovered specific changes in key regions in and around the hippocampus in the brains of young adults who were maltreated or neglected in childhood. These changes may leave victims more vulnerable to depression, addiction and PTSD.

Children with PTSD can have bad dreams, fear of dying, diminished interest in normal activities, more than normal headaches and stomach aches, trouble sleeping at night, intense irritability or increased anger or violent behavior. They can have trouble concentrating on any given task, and even demonstrate symptoms of clingy or whiny behavior.

When children with PTSD grow up, their symptoms may become much more subtle and harder to detect. As an adult, their symptoms can mimic other disorders such as anxiety, depression, and even reflect problems with drugs and alcohol. They can also experience problems with relationships and have a hard time trusting people.

### Other Effects of Abuse

In another study it was shown that abused children grow up to be more prone to cancer, obesity, heart disease, and depression as well as other health problems. They also discovered that the more severe the abuse and longer the duration, the more likely a child would develop many common life-threatening diseases (Gregg).

Experiencing trauma in childhood can have a severe and long-lasting effect. Children who have been traumatized see the world as a frightening and dangerous place. When childhood trauma is not resolved, this fundamental sense of fear and helplessness carries over into adulthood, setting the stage for further trauma.

That was me. I was an empty shell. I wanted to cry all the time. I got upset very easily over little things. I was very depressed all the time. The slightest failure on my part when trying to do anything would send me into a spiraling tailspin where I would wind up in an incredibly depressed state where the "demons" would literally haunt me for days. (To this day, this STILL can happen to me!) I felt like no matter what I tried to do, I would fail because of what everybody told me over and over and over so many times. I crumbled easily when confronted. I was extremely anxious about everything in life. I could not even talk on a phone. I was afraid of my own shadow. No matter where I went I imagined practically everyone I met had the potential to abuse me in some way. I was EXTREMELY afraid to let anybody inside. I was afraid to let anybody get that close to me. I did not want to get hurt anymore. I could not trust anybody. I felt like everybody could turn on me on a moment's notice. To this day I have a hard time with this.

There is a lot of suffering when dealing with PTSD. Trying to live in a world that constantly triggers you is extremely difficult. You have little control about how you feel or respond to a situation. The trauma is so entrenched that the reaction occurs before you even have time to think about it. Whenever someone expresses any kind of a negative reaction toward me, I instantly take it very personally and I become extremely upset. I always feel like they are intentionally harassing me or attempting to take advantage of me in some way. All of the old feelings come right back.

Along the pathway of growing up the "hoods" stole my childhood. I learned very early in life how ugly the world could be. Instead of enjoying the usual aspects of growing up like focusing on my academics at school and developing social connections, I was focusing on my next escape plan right after I got out of class to try to avoid the "hoods." Instead of developing great relationships with teachers, I would crawl into my private world for protection so that the teachers could not verbally abuse me anymore. Instead of enjoying my youth, I was forced to experience the cruel realities of life. Because of the "hoods," I lost my innocence.

Everywhere I went I was afraid that someone would find out about my past and either start treating me the same way by physically or emotionally abusing me, or look down and pity me. No matter where I went I was always afraid that someone would recognize me and know me from my past. I was a very nervous and scared young adult all of the time. I felt like I was totally worthless, with no self-esteem or confidence whatsoever. I was always very conscious that someone might start looking at me and stare at my deformities and become repulsed. I was a victim of PTSD because of my continued abuse while growing up.

### The Shadow Within

I learned early in life that no matter how hard I tried I could not win. No matter what it was — whether it was my schoolwork, my social life, or dealing with the "hoods," I was defeated. No matter what I did, nor how hard I tried to change the scenario, nothing worked. *Nothing* worked. I learned early-on what "hopelessness" felt like — what so many people in the world live and suffer with every day.

Because of what I suffered and endured, to this day, every time I make a mistake doing anything (such as misspell a word, make a carpentry mistake, or forget to do something), I can still hear the "hoods," administrators, and teachers telling me that I am a failure...I am no good...I cannot do anything right...Just give up!

Anytime I am around a pretty woman or a very successful, handsome man, I instantly feel like I am not worthy of being in their presence, much less even alive. I feel like I am nothing more than a piece of slime. Every time I get ready for a performance or direct a concert as a conductor I can hear the "hoods" getting ready to attack me ruthlessly. If I even miss only one note while I am performing, or miss one cue while conducting, the "demons" rush through my thoughts like a vengeance ready to destroy what I worked so hard to achieve. I always feel like the "demons" are just one step behind me ready on a moment's notice to obliterate anything I try to do right.

Because of my past, I have absolutely no patience for myself. I accept NO excuses for doing something wrong or without one-hundred percent effort from myself. To this day, I cannot even look at a mirror without total revulsion of what I see. This is what I was left with. This is what they did to me.

On the surface, most people around me would never know what I deal with every day. To a lot of people, I am a normal, confident professional. Because of the emotional and physical abuse I suffered, I also have a very destructive side to my personality. When my heart is going in and out of arrhythmia combined with the chemical changes in my brain from the lack of oxygen, I get extremely depressed and even suicidal. More than once, if it weren't for my strong faith, I would have committed suicide. As I look back on my life, the times I failed at anything were usually because I gave in to the "demons." I just gave up at whatever I was trying to achieve at that moment.

So why did I spend so much time talking about my childhood? I want you to understand what I have to deal with every day of my life. In a lot of ways, going to school while I was growing up and facing the physical and emotional abuse ON A DAILY BASIS was a lot like someone in the military going to battle every day. Facing that same turmoil day after day after day will change you forever. You will never be the same.

# Chapter 16
# Picking Up the Pieces; Facing My Fears

As I reflect on my life, I recognize certain times to have been key to my recovery from the many years of bullying I endured as a child. These are times when I was forced to face my fears and cope with difficult situations at hand. Facing those fears and being forced to deal with such situations enabled me to build inner strength that has stayed with me throughout my adult life. I believe that God placed me in those situations to help me become the person He intended me to be.

## *Working as a Food Store Bag Boy*

Late in my senior year of high school I knew I would soon be forced to face the adult world. I was petrified. But somewhere deep inside of me was a voice. It was a voice that kept telling me that there was more to my life, and that my life was just beginning. That voice kept telling me that He would protect me and help me find my way. I knew from early on that God had given me two strong gifts: one was in music and the other was stubbornness—

the fortitude to never give up. (I did not even know I had this gift until I was forced to use it.) I seemed to always know that my vehicle for success would be my music. What I did not know at the time, was how much musical talent God had given me. So for me, graduating from high school meant that I still had to develop the skills necessary for adulthood which I was unable to develop while growing up.

During that same year, I needed to earn money to purchase a car, pay for my flute lessons, and pay for gas, etc. I took a job as a bag boy at a local supermarket. Just at that time a new shopping plaza was built only three miles from my house. It included a food supermarket. So I applied as a bag boy and got the job.

I later found out that many of the "hoods" who tormented me in my junior high and high school years were currently working at the SAME store on a full-time basis. Most of them had finally quit school without graduating. Several of them had gotten married, started having children and had to go to work at lower level jobs because of their lack of a high school diploma.

I did not realize that the "hoods" were working at the same store until after the first month I was employed. They usually clocked out before I clocked in. At first I didn't think they recognized me. I was a lot taller. I had grown to my present height of almost five foot, eleven inches. But slowly they began to realize I was the same kid they used to beat up. For the most part they left me alone as long as I stayed out of their way. They basically kept to themselves. If they saw me in the back stock room they might walk up to me and just push me aside as they walked out. When I first saw them I was terrified. All of the old horrible feelings started to come back to me. When I first realized they were there, I threw up I was so scared. But I could not avoid them. I actually had to work beside them on many occasions. As scared as I was, I wanted to keep my part-time job as a bag boy, so I dealt with it and forced myself to confront them every day I worked.

It was interesting to note that they carried a different demeanor about them at that point. It was more like they had been defeated or humbled. They would look down as they walked by me trying not to look me in the eye. Had the chip on their shoulders been knocked off by the toughness and pains of life? Eventually some of these "hoods" actually began to make small talk with me. They discovered I was a human being and I likewise discovered that they had *some* human traits also.

By the time I was getting ready to graduate from high school, and I had been working at the food store for over a year, some of the "hoods" had accepted me into their inner circles. I even hung out after work with a select few of them! Some of them even offered to help me find "chicks." But even when I occasionally socialized with some of them, I realized that I could never be one of them. Getting drunk, getting into fights and trying to pick up girls was not my idea of a good time. One of them even offered to help me out if I ever got picked on. He said that he would "take care of them" for me. By the time I started college the next fall, some of the "hoods" were even asking me about what it was like to go to college. None of them had even completed high school. I realize now how that experience helped me to confront my fears, draw strength from it, and become a stronger person.

Several years later while I was on the road as a touring musician, I went into that same food store to buy groceries for my parents when I was visiting them. I noticed that many of the same "hoods" were *still* working at the same food store doing the exact same work and driving the same cars. By then we were all more than ten years older. I felt a sense of satisfaction knowing that I had moved ahead in life and they were still trapped in the same exact place where they were ten years earlier. Maybe in a small way, I won the battle! Despite what I had suffered under them, I was able to move on with my life.

## *Middle School Band Director*

One of the toughest jobs for me that helped me to face my fears from the years of abuse was a position I accepted as a band director at an inner city school system. Many schools in the middle Georgia area were considered some of the most violent places to work at the time. Because of so much school violence at a high school in Macon (Georgia), the band director's salary was one of the highest in the Southeast. The band director that worked there jokingly called his supplemental salary "combat pay." The school I was hired at was a middle school that looked like a war zone. I accepted the position because I wanted a job that was in the same town, or close by where I lived. When I interviewed for the position all of the old feelings I had when I was in junior high school started coming back to me. The school environment reminded me of my junior high experience. In spite of that, I accepted the position and hoped that I could overcome those old feelings.

Over the course of several months as I was working, I began to get even more apprehensive. There was so much violence at the school that they even hired a paraprofessional to help control it. He was an ex-football player, hired to help stop the fighting. Violence was rampant. There were probably several fights every day. Many of them were extremely brutal. Some students ended up in the hospital. Even though this was a middle school, many of the students were in their middle to late teens. They were grown men. They brought various weapons such as knives and guns. Drugs were rampant. To make matters worse, if a faculty member saw a fight it was their responsibly to break it up. If they did not they could lose their job or even be sued. I was terrified! Every one of my old feelings came back with a vengeance. I was reliving my past.

I focused on doing my work as best as I could. But I could not avoid the fights. They would happen around me anywhere, anytime. Fights could break out in my band room, in the hallway as I was walking through, or anywhere on the school campus. It did not take long before the ultimate horror happened to me. I had to break up a fight. It started right in front of me as I was walking to another building. Two boys easily twice my size, were going at it. There was blood everywhere. These boys were trying to kill each other. I yelled at them but they didn't stop. As I stood there watching I could not help but think about all the beatings I had endured. I could feel every punch as if it were directed at me. At that moment I realized that enough was enough. I jumped in between them and tried to pull them apart. As I grabbed one of them the other kept trying to hit the other boy. I had to grab him also. After what seemed like minutes, help arrived.

Once everything calmed down the boys were taken to the principal's office and then escorted to the hospital for treatment. As I was walking back to the band room I realized that this may be some kind of therapy for me to help me face my fears. I had to physically stop fights during my band classes, disarm students who were carrying weapons, and constantly be on the lookout for students passing drugs. I stayed at that job for five years and built a very successful band program in spite of it all. At the time I resigned to begin work on my doctorate degree, I was sending close to one hundred students a year to the high school band program. I had to break up fights regularly during my years at that school. In a strange way I DO believe that it was therapy for me to face those fears again. I did face them and built a superior band program despite the violence.

### The Job Was Mine — Or So I Thought

After I completed my doctoral degree in 1998, I applied for a position as the jazz director at the university near my home town in Georgia. I was already on the music faculty working as a Senior

Lecturer, teaching flute, conducting the jazz combo, and teaching other music courses. Over the course of several weeks I made it through the usual series of rounds of elimination until finally I was one of three selected to go through the final on-campus interview process. After I went through the grueling two day process of demonstrations of my teaching and performance abilities and attending several meetings, I felt reasonably good about my chances of getting the position.

Well, when all was said and done, I was not selected. I was told that I had come in second. I was shocked! I thought that I had a very good chance of being selected based on my education, experience and performance qualifications. What this meant was that in order for me to work full-time as a college professor, we would have to move, probably out of state. To teach at a university, you go where the jobs are. They are extremely competitive and there are very few openings. I was devastated. I went into one of the biggest depressions I had had in several years. My "demons" went on the warpath, laughing and telling me, "I told you so!" To make matters even worse when looking for a college position most jobs only come available during the nine month school year for the next fall. Since this interview took place late in the spring, the chances were not very good that anything that I would qualify for would come open for the next school year. I was about as low as I could go.

All of the old "demons" were having a field day with me. I was even having suicidal thoughts because of my heart problem. I was numb for most of the rest of the spring and summer. The "demons" were winning — or so they thought.

At that point I was totally confused. I had recently completed my doctoral degree. I was working at two colleges as an adjunct professor while maintaining a fabulous *huge* flute studio in my home (with over forty-five private students). I was picking up music jobs (playing flute and bass guitar) all around the Middle-Georgia area. I was doing very well. And then this happened. I was mortified. I was extremely depressed, more than I had been since I was a child. Being an adult, I had already experienced many disappointments in my life. But I think this one hit me so hard because it involved the gift that God had given me—the gift of music. Here I had finally reached the pinnacle of my education only to be disappointed with no job prospect in my home area in Georgia.

Well, instead of giving up, I reached down deep into my soul and talked to God. I did not understand what He wanted out of me at that time, but I was willing to listen to Him on what direction to take from there. I prayed, my wife prayed, and we prayed together on what to do next. Slowly I began to realize that my future was not in Middle Georgia. God wanted me to start fresh somewhere new.

What I did not know at that time, was that God had decided that I needed to go out of state for my full-time college position. By doing so I would be able to find doctors that would help me with my heart and other continuous health problems. My wife contends that I would not be alive today if it weren't for the doctors who treated me in Nebraska and Iowa. By moving, my mother-in-law found and remarried a retired gentleman farmer. (She was living with us in Georgia and came up to the Midwest with us.) Furthermore, both of my sons attended and graduated from the university I would teach at. I also learned later that both of my sons benefitted highly in many other ways by our moving. My wife and I would also start a Christian musical ministry in the Midwest.

So, after talking to my family, we decided that I would look for a full-time college position out of state during the next school year, which meant I had to make a living doing what I was currently doing for yet another year. As I secured my adjunct teaching appointments for another year, the chairman of the music department of the university where I did not get the full-time position, was surprised that I would want to work there after what happened. I told him I needed the job for another year. He agreed for the upcoming year. I ended up having to work beside the person who got the job for that entire year. That was the hardest thing I had to do. Of course, I realized that he had nothing to do with my not getting the job, but I still had quite a bit of resentment toward him.

While I worked there I often encountered the chairman of the music department. He happened to be the individual who made the final decision on who to hire. Many times we would be cordial and make some attempt at small talk. Finally late into the spring, he met me in the hallway and made an extremely profound statement to me. He said that he could not have worked there that year if it had been him. He said that I was one of the strongest persons he had ever known. He said that he could not have done it. (I later found out that the other candidate was chosen only because they wanted someone who was primarily a single reed player. My first instrument was the flute.) After he left, I stood there stunned. For what seemed like several minutes, I just stood there and reflected on what he had just said. I realized that I had beaten my "demons." I had defeated my past (or at least kept it at bay). I was able to work through life's turmoil and rise above it. I was energized. I worked hard and eventually secured a full-time university faculty position out of state for the next year.

# Chapter 17
## God is Always with Us

No matter who you are or what you've been through in your life, it's important to remember that God is always with you. He always has been. We can't explain *why* bad things happen to us, or how God could allow violence or harmful events or tragedies. We just know that God loves us all, and has good plans for each and every one of us. Remember the story of Joseph (Genesis, Chapters 37-50). Joseph was a *good* person, yet he was subjected to abandonment, slavery and imprisonment when he was innocent. Yet in the end, he triumphed. If the story of Joseph is examined, God never revealed Himself directly to Joseph, yet many people who knew Joseph recognized that God was with him.

So too is God with you, even if you feel abandoned. We have no way of understanding God's plan, explaining why we have to endure hard times, or knowing what our futures will bring. But rest assured that God loves you and wants the best for you. He wants to see you bloom and thrive despite obstacles in your life. You too can triumph in the end. If I can do it, so can you.

My wife often states that I'm a very "guarded" person, meaning that God is with me, watching out for me throughout my life. All of this is in spite of the turmoil I've endured. The following are some examples of things that have happened to me that we feel is evidence of God's presence in my life.

## *Potential Holdup*

A turning point in my life occurred when I was involved in a potential holdup. Back when I was just starting my band right after graduating from high school, we used to practice in the back of my dad's hardware store after hours. One night after we were finished and heading out the door we noticed some guys, probably just a few years older than us, staring in the store windows and just generally hanging around. Since most of us lived next door to each other we rode to the store in one car. So after we all got into the car we drove off but decided to circle around and see what those other guys were up to. We were concerned that they were casing the stores to burglarize later.

As I pulled the car up to my dad's store one of the men we were watching walked over to my side of the car (I was driving). He motioned for me to roll down my window. As I put the car into park and rolled my window down, he raised his hand and put a pistol to the left side of my head. He then demanded for the three of us in the car to hand over all our valuables or he was going to shoot me. At first I was stunned! This did not seem real. As I was thinking about my situation I did feel the coldness of the pistol against my temple. As I was contemplating what to do next, our drummer, who was in the backseat of the car, belted out to the gunmen that his gun was not real. After the drummer's comment, the gunman raised his gun to the air and fired it, and then instantly put it back to my head. At that moment I finally came to the realization that this *was* for real. Strangely, I was not scared. I was able to talk to the gunman in a calm, even voice despite the fact that the gun was still being held against my temple. I felt a presence and was not scared. I felt like I was going to be OK.

We kept trying to explain to the gunman that we were starving musicians and had no money, which was true. By that time, the other two men had walked over to my car. They started talking to the gunman, acting very nervously, telling him to quit wasting his time with us and that they needed to leave. At that moment one of the men threw something in our car and all three of them jumped into their car and left. As they left, we realized we had some kind of mace or smoke bomb in my car. As they sped away in their car we all jumped out of my car and tried to assess what had just happened.

Once we collected our thoughts we ran to the end of the strip mall (about one block) and called the police. Within one or two minutes, I estimate over fifty police/state trooper/deputy sheriff cars came screeching into the parking lot. Once we explained which way the "hoods" had gone, most of their cars took off after them. After several minutes one of the troopers explained to us what was going on.

About an hour earlier three men held up and killed one of the employees at a convenience store a few miles from us. The men that tried to hold us up, fit the description exactly. After a few more minutes, another trooper walked over to us scratching his head, and said that he could not explain why none of us were injured or killed. He said that these were desperate criminals who had nothing to lose. He said that my guardian angel must have been watching over me. This event helped to push and inspire me to do more with my life. I no longer took life for granted and began to treasure every moment I had on Earth.

## *The Hitchhiker*

An unusual event happened to me when my brother, our two neighborhood friends, and I decided to drive from Tampa down to Sarasota to have some fun on the beach. As we approached the city limits of Sarasota we noticed a young man, possibly in his early twenties, walking on the side of the road. He indicated that he needed a ride. We stopped and asked him what was wrong. He said that his car had broken down a few miles back and needed a ride to get to town. Since there were four guys in the car, we thought we should be alright picking up a hitchhiker.

Once in the car he was extremely quiet and seemed very nervous. He kept placing his hand in his backpack and looking around at each of us. The four of us were trying to make small talk asking him where he lived and what his car looked like. We had just driven down the road where he said his car was supposedly stopped, and didn't recall seeing any such car. About that time we started to get a little nervous too. As we made a turn we noticed that there was a police blockade up ahead. Since the cars were backed up, we had to stop.

When we stopped, the hitchhiker excused himself and jumped out of the car and ran off. When we got to the point where the blockade was, we asked the police officer what they were looking for. They informed us that they were looking for an escaped criminal who was wanted for murder and other serious crimes. He was considered heavily armed and very dangerous. The description he gave matched our hitchhiker. After talking to the policeman and telling him about the hitchhiker, we just looked at each other and did not say another word until we were at the beach. Apparently the hitchhiker was armed and could have killed us all or forced us to leave the car, while he stole it. Instead we were left unharmed and safe. Again, it appears that I was being looked after by God.

### *"David, wake up!"*

There was another time I felt the presence of God in a very profound way. When I was living in Georgia, I was driving back from a music job. Typically the band would play until 1:00 or 2:00 o'clock in the morning, load the equipment, and then head home. I usually had one of the vans to be loaded. Well, by the time we were loaded up it was usually 2:00 to 3:00AM, Sunday morning. To make matters worse it was often a two to three hour drive to get home. On this one fateful early morning my heart was doing its intermittent arrhythmia dance and I was extremely tired. Plus, I was taking heart medications that made me feel lethargic.

I was about an hour from home when I had to pass through a small town. As I was driving through the town on Main Street, I fell asleep. My body just gave out. I don't know how long I was asleep when somebody grabbed my shoulder, and in a very stern voice said, "David, wake up!" (I was the only person in the car.) Of course I woke up with a sudden jerk. As I looked up I realized I was less than ten feet from driving through the front window of a department store. Apparently while I was asleep, I had driven several hundred feet, missed a turn, and ended up driving right up to a department store. I immediately slammed on my brakes and came to a stop less than a few feet from the window. As I sat in my seat I thought about what had just happened. After a few minutes of prayers I was able to drive home.

### *Stranded in a Tuxedo*

In yet another apparently divine encounter, I was scheduled to be the guest soloist during the Mercer University Wind Ensemble spring concert. The event was to be at the Grand Opera House located in downtown Macon, Georgia. Shortly before this event I had inherited an older Cadillac and drove it when I had to transport my entire family (two young sons, my wife, my mother and mother-in-law). We lived about an hour south of Macon in a city called Warner Robins. Everything was fine until I was about five miles from the opera house. All of a sudden the car stopped running as we were driving off the interstate. We made it off the exit ramp and onto the road, near a major intersection. We saw a gas station nearby that was closed. It was a Sunday afternoon. We started to push the car to the gas station and fortunately, many kind souls saw us and offered their help. After getting the car off the road and in the gas station lot, we were perplexed as to what to do at that point. Here I was in a tuxedo, needing to get to my destination to play as the featured soloist and I was stranded with five other family members!

Then it happened. Something none of us had ever seen before. A woman, alone in her car, pulled up in a GOLD Mercedes Benz. With a serious look on her face, she looked right at me (and no one else) and asked, "Do YOU need a ride?" I was stunned. She wasn't addressing her offer to the entire family — just to ME. I hesitated. She said again, in a somewhat firm voice, "Do YOU need a ride?" I looked at my wife and family and they all said, "Go." I felt bad leaving all my family stranded behind on the street. But they urged me to go; so I did.

The entire way there, she never looked at me and didn't change her demeanor, nor did she offer any small talk. I attempted to make conversation with her, but she remained silent. She took me to my destination, safe and sound. I thanked her and she drove off, still without saying a word. By the grace of God, I was able to warm up properly and perform as the featured soloist in the concert.

In the meantime, my oldest son, who had his cell phone, called a cab to carry the rest of my family to the opera house. They made it in time for the concert. Then he got busy calling friends, who were kind enough to come get us all. It took TWO cars to come get us, each with about an hour drive to get there! In the meantime our old Cadillac was being towed back to Warner Robins.

### Black Ice

And, here's yet another incident where there was apparent divine intervention that probably saved my life. I was driving very early one Sunday morning (about 6:30AM) to attend a church praise band rehearsal before the 8:30AM service. The roads appeared to be clear with no snow. It was winter in Iowa. As I was driving out of town there was a series of sharp twists and turns while going up a steep hill leaving town. As I was almost to the turns I had to drive over a bridge. As soon as I got to the bridge there was a herd of deer standing right in the middle of the road. Normally I would be driving about 45 miles per hour as I was heading up the hill. But I had to come to a complete stop, and then go slowly around the deer. After I passed them, I started up the hill at a much slower speed than normal.

As I approached the last turn, I hit some black ice. Instantly my car started spinning numerous times. Fortunately, my car spun inward toward the side of the hill. If my car had spun toward the outside of the curve, I would have gone over the side of the hill with a fifty foot drop into a valley area. When my car hit the gravel on the inside of the road, it rolled several times. As it rolled, I remember my head constantly being slammed against the driver's window. The car finally landed on the passenger side.

I was knocked out for what seemed like minutes. When I came to, I checked myself and saw that I was still buckled in my seat belt. I unlocked my seatbelt and then fell to the passenger side of the car. I then realized the car was still running and the headlights were on. I reached up, turned the car off, and pulled myself up to my driver's seat and climbed out of the window. As I was standing on the driver's side door I looked at my poor car and saw that all the windows were broken and the car was twisted like a pretzel. At that point I jumped off the car to the ground. As I jumped I realized how dark it was since the sun had not come up yet.

As soon as I hit the ground I heard a voice asking me if I was OK. I turned around to see a woman in a car that had just come down the hill. Somehow she did not hit any black ice with her car. As I looked back at my car I noticed that it was smoking and one of the wheels was still spinning. She immediately offered me a ride and took me back to town so I could call the police. For some reason I did not hesitate. I walked over to her car and she took me straight back into town.

My wife was running her bakery at the time and was working in the kitchen (by necessity) that morning. When I walked in, I told her I just wrecked the car. At first, she thought I was joking. It didn't take long though, for her to realize that I was very serious. She immediately made me sit down and called the police. She explained to them that I had left the scene of the accident for the purpose of making the phone call. THAT's when we learned that there had been a second accident in the exact same place. Only this time, things were much more serious.

The second car spun around and rolled in such a way that it almost hit my car. AND, as my wife was told by the police attendant on the phone, if I had stood by my car as I probably would have, the second car would probably have hit me and likely killed me. As it turned out, I was perfectly fine, aside from some cuts and bruises. The driver of the second car wasn't wearing his seatbelt and was thrown around quite a bit during the accident. My wife took me to the hospital to be checked out and also to meet the police there. When we arrived, we found the medical helicopter there, waiting for the other driver to be transported to a larger city for medical treatment. He died on the way.

The next day I went to the junk yard where they towed my poor little car, so I could claim any papers or personal items that were still in the car. As I looked at my navy blue Chevy Blazer, I still did not see how I walked away from it. It looked like an accordion and twisted pretzel all rolled into one. Every window had shattered and even the A-frame was twisted. And yet somehow, I literally walked away unhurt. Again, was it divine intervention that the lady who stopped just *happened* to be there to help me at that early hour on a Sunday morning? I know better than to leave the scene of an accident, but I was so stunned and in shock that all I could think about was going home to my wife. The two accidents happened so close together in time, it's speculated that as I was being taken down the hill back to town, we probably passed the other driver as he was going up the hill. Had I stood by my car, as I most likely would have done to wait for the police, I probably would have gotten killed by the other car spinning out of control. Was my guardian angel looking out for me once again?

### Money from Heaven

Most recently, my wife and I started our Christian music ministry with the goal of inspiring others to use their God-given gifts. We learned of a newly released movie "The Bible" and I was especially interested in buying it. I told my wife about it and took her to a local store where the movie was being sold. It was rather expensive and our money was tight at the time. Judi also wanted the movie, but was concerned about spending that much at the moment for such an item. I found the movie and took it to her when she was elsewhere in the store. She expressed her concern about finances and suggested we go look at the display. I had the intention of putting the movie back on the shelf.

On the way to the display I didn't notice anything on the floor, but Judi happened to see me step right over money. She picked it up. It was a new $50 bill folded in half. She looked around and saw no one nearby. She would have returned it to its rightful owner, but since no one was around, there was no way of knowing who had dropped it. She was astounded! She instantly considered it to be a gift from God so I could purchase the movie. We discussed the possibilities of trying to find out who may have dropped the money, but realized that would be impossible. Imagine how many people would show up at customer service claiming to have dropped cash! Without hesitation, we went straight to the register and purchased the movie. Did someone lose $50 that day or was it divine intervention? We don't know for certain, but my wife is sure it was a gift from God so I could see the movie.

# Chapter 18
# One Step at a Time —
# Unlocking the Person Inside

Even though I did not realize it at the time, God was guiding me throughout my life. He gave me the will to not quit. Inside me was an incredible thirst to learn. I was literally starving for all the things I had missed in my younger years. To bring out the person I was meant to be, He started by giving me a series of small steps throughout my everyday life, either through my college school work, my music, or dealing with life in general. I had to gain self-esteem, confidence, and the ability to interact with other people in assorted situations. I had to *learn* how to achieve success. The steps God placed before me were very small at first, but over time with what He asked of me, those first steps forced me to learn how to achieve greater and greater successes. By doing this He slowly made me into a new person who was being filled with more confidence, acceptance, compassion, and even more patience for myself.

He then put me in situations where my back was literally against the wall, where I had nowhere to go but up. Many times because I was so naive, I had no idea what I was getting into. Whether it was in some academic or music classes, performances, or adult situations, I had to fight. I had to learn. I had to move forward. I had no choice. Something inside of me would not let me quit—not anymore. I learned how to become a fighter. God was on my side! He was my rock. I could lean against Him whenever I starting getting weak. When I was younger I was knocked down literally hundreds of times either physically or emotionally. I was used to being knocked down, but somehow I learned how to get back up each and every time. Over time I learned how to NEVER give up, no matter what I was facing.

After the little successes, larger successes started to enter my life. God gave me larger tasks, like teaching private lessons, managing my first bands, working with booking agents and night club owners, etc. Through all of this I started to feel like a real person. I even started to feel fairly good about myself some of the time. That was when God decided to kick my rebuilding up to a higher level.

When I got the call from the management agency about taking my band on the road touring full-time, I knew that my training was going to go into "full throttle." While on the road, I had no one to help me deal with all the problems that came along with touring. My dad would not be there to help me, my local business associates that I could always ask for advice when in a pinch would not be there either. I had to step up to the plate. My back was against the wall. It seems God always works that way to get me to do anything new. We performed in multi-million dollar resort hotels and clubs up and down the East Coast. I had to deal with corrupt booking agencies, crooked night club owners, pimps, prostitutes, bad club patrons, and even misbehaving musicians in my own band. It was the best education I could ever have gotten.

# SECTION V
# How God Has Shaped and Used Me

# Chapter 19
# God's Plan for Me;
# God's Plan for You

I know that God's gift literally saved me. My gift of music brought me out of the life of despair that I was forced into from the "hoods." My gift gave me the purpose, motivation and reason to live and move forward. Without my musical gift from God, I would not be here today. I could not have survived the many years of abuse without my music. Music was the driving force that kept me wanting to get up and go to school every day, despite knowing that I would have to deal with the "hoods." Music was the catalyst that made me what I am today.

I know that God has the power to heal me. Instead He has chosen to use me as I am, with all my health problems and physical afflictions, to spread His Word to everyone through my music and testimony. I teach music by example. As a child of God, I use my music as a way to bring Christ into the lives of my students by the way I treat them, talk to them, work with them, and help them on their way to becoming young adults.

I would not be what I am today without having experienced all the pain and suffering and turmoil in my life. I learned a lot about myself going through the dark days of growing up. I am a survivor! My past life has made me much stronger. Now with God's help, I can achieve anything I give one-hundred percent to. James 1:12 reminds us that "Blessed is the man who perseveres under trial, because when he has stood the test, he will receive the crown of life that God has promised to those who love Him."

Can I forgive all of the people who abused me when I was growing up? I don't know, but I'm working on it. I know I could never forget my past abuse. I have worked on moving ahead with my life. In doing so, I try to fill my central thoughts and memories with the positive outcomes and experiences I have had. The more I move ahead with my life the further back those abusive memories become. Those memories are no longer in the forefront of my existence.

Corinthians 10:13 states: "No temptation has overtaken you that is not common to man. God is faithful, and He will not let you be tempted beyond your ability, but with the temptation He will also provide the way of escape, that you may be able to endure it." I know now that God will not give me any task larger than I can handle. With God's help I learned just how far I could push myself both physically and mentally. I've learned that with God's help, I can do almost anything. I've also learned that without God, I cannot accomplish anything. I have already accomplished much more in my life than I could have ever imagined. Again, God is not going to test you nor tempt you beyond what you can bear, so be encouraged to know that whatever you're going through, He will always be there to help you overcome it.

Currently I am a full-time college professor teaching flute, jazz, and recording technology. I also perform as principal flutist in a regional orchestra and a professional concert band, in addition to being the band's assistant conductor. I give flute and jazz clinics all over the Midwest. I currently have a small private flute studio where I teach lessons to children ranging from elementary school through high school age. I have the great honor of shaping young minds using the power of God through my music.

Because of my past, I seem to understand children when I work with them. I feel very comfortable around them. I can relate to them, and seem to understand what they are experiencing at any point in their young lives. I have tremendous patience and apathy for them. I typically start young flute students in elementary school and they almost always continue with me through high school. I have even started lessons with flute students at the tender age of five!

As children of God, I realize how important it is to guide and nurture them spiritually as they grow up. I try to be a role model and a positive influence on them. I don't want them to suffer the same abuse I had to endure. All children are God's children. I never forget that. I understand the underdog. I understand the weak. I will do anything I possibly can to help them get on their feet and move forward with their young lives. I can share their pain. I am one of them.

Hardships have made me stronger, much stronger. Now I look at hardships as a personal challenge. I get excited about starting something new, whether it is learning new recording or video editing software, or how to operate a new video camera, or writing this book. I even started and introduced a whole new degree program in recording technology at the university where I teach. We now have as many music production majors as music majors. I even started and completed a fourth degree in recording technology after I began working as a professor at my current college position. There is growth from personal hardships and challenges, and I look to them in a positive way now rather than negative.

I believe that I can achieve whatever I put my mind to do, no matter what others around me say. I have achieved what others said I could not. That alone has given me inner strength beyond words. No matter what your personal hell has been, you too have worth. You are beautiful in God's eyes. God has a plan for you and you can draw strength from your past. You're a survivor. Move forward and fulfill God's plan for your life.

I often wondered if I could ever recover from the trauma I received as a child. But now as I look back, God outlined a plan for me to achieve many wonderful things and even more. It can also happen to you. Yes, recovery is possible. But you already know you can't just snap your fingers and make everything better overnight. It took me over twenty years to turn my life around. There are two very important truths to remember as you start your journey toward a new life. *You are not alone*, and *there is hope*.

Your recovery will be a process of learning and remembering those two truths, not just once, but over and over. As I started the journey to my recovery I had to tell myself *every day*, that I *could* achieve what I strived for and be a success. Yes, you may have been hurt, but with God's help and guidance, you too can create a new you!

Abuse does not have to "stamp" you. You can change. God gave you a different identity. No matter what terrible atrocities happened to you, they are not your identity. Your identity as God's child is far deeper than the abuse you suffered. When you come to God through trusting in Jesus, He gives you a new identity, the "*you*" He intended to be. You become part of the family of God. You are his dearly loved child.

The abuse you suffered is part of the stage upon which your life choices will now take place. It's out of the choices you are facing right now that great goodness can come. That doesn't mean that you will forget the evil done to you. But now you can use that force to create new and wonderful things for the glory of God. You also can choose how to respond to the evil that was done to you. You can grow in gratitude, joy, purpose, and the ability to help others and live your life with courage and conscious intent. You too can achieve what you put your mind to do. If you *believe* that you can do something, you *can* do it. Believe in yourself. God does, so you should too.

Remember the old adage: "Inch by inch, it's a cinch. Yard by yard, it's hard." Break down your large goals and ambitions into small milestones and work on them one at a time. Once a step is achieved, pat yourself on the back for that accomplishment, and move forward. If you encounter stumbling blocks, consider them to be God's way of diverting you toward the path that you *should* be on, not where you were headed. When one door is shut in front of you, another will open. God has great plans for you and He will guide you along the way. Trust in God and His plan for you.

A teacher once told me I would never be able to graduate from high school. *Now*, I've not only graduated from high school, but I have *four* college degrees, culminating with an earned doctoral degree! Now I *teach* college students, as well as private music students who have ranged from five through eighty-one years of age. Some of my former students have gone on to earn *their* doctoral degrees in flute performance and some are playing professionally in orchestras. Praise God!

# Chapter 20
# Small Steps I Use to
# Beat My "Demons"

My music started me on my journey to recovery. God saved me through my music! God gave me the gift of music and through it I learned how to turn my life around and move forward. Learning music is all about macro (large) and micro (small) practicing techniques, being organized, working toward goals, building one success after another, and working together with other musicians. By using the same formula and applying it to everything else I tried to accomplish in my life, I achieved success. I started this process in my late teens and am still developing and refining it today. Everything I have accomplished in my life is either a direct or indirect result of my musical gift. Find *your* gift and it could also help you overcome your troubled past. Your gift will help you on your way to a happier and more fulfilling life.

The following are simple principals that I use every day of my life. They help to keep me moving forward and achieving the tasks that are before me. You too can apply these same principals to help overcome the obstacles in *your* life.

**Take one moment at a time.** I take my life one moment at a time. When I have something to do or finish, I try to focus on the task at hand and not think of the future. I'll have my schedule of things I need to do but I will only focus on what I have scheduled at the moment in order to keep me organized and on task. Because of my ADHD, if I try to multi-task, I end up drifting away from what I should be doing and not completing it.

**Focus on the "now" and not the "what ifs."** I try to focus on the moment instead of the "what ifs" in life. For example, what if I do poorly in a performance? Or, what if I fail an exam of some kind? Every time I focus on the "what ifs," I fail at whatever it is I am trying to accomplish. In my case, the "what ifs" always open the door for my "demons." Now I map out a plan of action — a series of large and small steps. Then I work toward that goal one small step at a time, no matter how much work it may take.

**Organize your time.** Each and every day of my life is broken down into various routines and schedules. If I don't do it that way, I immediately start procrastinating and I accomplish little to nothing. My schedule becomes a regular routine, so I can accomplish everything I need to do. This applies to exercising, practicing my music, preparing for a lecture, or any task that must be completed regularly. I do my best to stay with that routine. Even if I have a performance coming up in the next several weeks I work backward from the performance date and map out my entire rehearsal schedule so that I am on task regarding learning the music. I learned long ago, that the tighter and more organized my scheduling, the better I succeed at whatever task I am working toward. I have broken my life up into many segments.

**Break large tasks into small steps and realize your accomplishments as you finish each step.** I think of life as a series of mountains. Every day I climb a few more steps up the mountain, and then the next day, and the next day, etc. After a day of climbing up the mountain, I'll congratulate myself on the day's accomplishments and tackle the next part of the journey the next day. I NEVER think of the whole journey at one time. I tackle everything I do one step at a time. If I am about to tackle something new I write out a series of macro and micro schedules and steps to get me through the given project. Once I have it all mapped out I focus and work ONLY on the required work for that day. I don't worry about the unfinished work that lay ahead of me. I only focus on what is at hand. I used this technique to complete my doctoral degree over a six year period.

While I was working on my doctoral degree, I was also working at two universities as an adjunct professor, working as a freelance professional musician in two different bands, performing in recording studios and orchestras, and teaching forty private students. I had everything so detailed that I knew six months in advance what was going on in my life and what I was supposed to do at that time.

**Recognize your successes.** I look at every little endeavor I *complete* as a success. It does not matter how small a task it was that I completed, I think of it as a success. This applies not only to major tasks, but to everyday life activities such as mowing the grass, teaching a class, or practicing my flute. I use *each* success as a way to fuel my confidence and keep away the negative feelings. I constantly congratulate myself on every successful completion. One of my goals is to achieve a series of successes *every day* by the time I go to bed at night.

**Finish everything you start.** I developed the stubbornness to never quit anything I started, no matter how small or trivial it may seem to me or anybody else. Again, it does not matter what it is I have started. It could be maintenance on the house, or working on the yard or car. I always force myself to finish the task, even if it takes weeks (and sometimes years) to do so. It usually becomes an obsession with me. Quitting is a habit that I started in my childhood as a result of being told over and over that I was no good and should just quit and give up. After years of abuse, I was living out what I was told. But once I got out of high school, I knew I had to stop that pattern. I had to break the cycle. I noticed that anytime I quit something I had started, I soon found myself procrastinating on other things, and would not complete *anything* I had started. Every time I started to procrastinate, it opened up the doors for the "demons." The "demons" would then start attacking me, giving me the same old "song" that I am worthless and no good and should just quit! Once the "demons" started to work on me, I would usually give up and not complete the task at hand. I learned to build upon every success I had so that if I did fail at something, I used my previous successes to draw upon to keep me going until I achieved my next success.

**Reward yourself for your achievements.** I use the reward method after achieving successes in my life. For instance, when I was in graduate school working on my master's degree, I would make myself study really hard for a particular test. Then afterwards I would treat myself to a dollar movie theatre that was in town. While working on my doctoral degree, I would reward myself with a food treat or a walk around the mall after a stressful test or performance. I still treat myself after a performance.

**Remind yourself of your achievements.** In my office at the college where I teach, I have hung pictures of many of my performances over the years. Most people who see them, think that I hung them to show everyone what I have accomplished and all of the different musicians I have worked with during my career. While I do enjoy sharing my career with everyone, the main reason I hung them is to remind myself of the many successes I have accomplished over the years. This actually helps me when, on some days, the "demons" are trying to break through and ruin my day. When I am feeling blue, I look around my office and remind myself about the successes I have had. That helps me to fight off the "demons" and negative thoughts.

**Don't be afraid to try something new.** I have forced myself to do things where I had no idea what I was getting into. I have forced myself to try things that were totally new to me, such as writing this book. I used to look at tackling something new with pure panic. Now I look forward to the challenge.

When my wife and I bought a 10,000 square foot commercial building I had to do most of the remodeling. The problem was I had never done any construction nor electrical wiring (other than helping my father, who was an electrician). Once we purchased the building I immediately bought books and videos on the tasks at hand. I also asked a lot of questions from experts in the various construction fields. I ended up totally gutting all three floors and built a 2,300 square foot, two bedroom apartment complete with a beautiful kitchen, bathroom and gas fireplace on the top floor, a commercial kitchen and restaurant on the main floor, and a 1,700 square foot commercial recording studio in the basement. What a learning endeavor *that* was! Now when I am faced with something brand new to learn, I am always excited and look forward to the challenge.

**Realize that you can't do everything like a pro. Accept your limitations.** To this day I cannot spell. This is one of the biggest drawbacks from my dissociation in school because of my abuse while growing up. Of all the things I had to overcome, spelling is the one area I have struggled with my entire life. I do my best and usually have access to a dictionary or the internet. I have accepted the fact that my doctoral degree is in music, not English. I try not to be hard on myself if I make a spelling mistake.

**Do NOT quit!** I have often gotten myself into situations (many times deliberately) that were way over my head. But because of my stubbornness, I would not quit. This forced me to go through the long process of learning new things and achieving success.

When somebody tells me that I cannot do something because I don't have the necessary skills, training, or general smarts, I become enraged. While growing up I was told *many* times by my teachers, fellow students, administrators, and the "hoods" that I was not good enough to accomplish or learn anything.

Now when someone tells me I cannot do something, I *find* a way to do it. The more they insist that I cannot do it, the more I am determined to overcome whatever obstacle there may be so I *can* complete the task. I absolutely refuse to accept the notion that I cannot successfully complete something. Anytime negative energy is thrown upon me by someone or some situation, I change that negative energy into positive energy so I can accomplish what I need to do at that moment.

**Give it your "all."** I usually give one-hundred percent of my energy and time to everything I do, and complete tasks the best I can. While I was growing up I failed at most things because of the "demons" telling me to give up. Because of that fact I usually put out minimal effort and often failed. I have since learned that if I give one-hundred percent to any endeavor no matter what it is, I am able to successfully complete it. I refuse to accept any less effort out of myself! I do not want the "demons" to charge up the hill screaming at me about my failures. I will not give them a chance to harass me anymore. Failure is not an option with me!

**Look for inspiration from others.** I am always trying to read about people who had to overcome adverse problems in their lives. They are my inspiration to keep going. If they were able to overcome their problems, then I can overcome mine. I like to feed off of their energy.

**Remember the positive things in your life and that you are loved.** I still have days where I feel like a failure. Anything can trigger the "demons" and negative thoughts. Even a snaring glance toward me or an unkind word can trigger them. Everyone has them. But, mixing an unkind remark with my heart arrhythmia can trigger incredible depression. When I get depressed, the whole world turns dark to me. Visually everything seems dark grey and drab. I can get so depressed that I have been suicidal many times. I never want to hurt anybody else, only myself because of my past. When my heart is acting up I can reach the very bottom of my limits of sanity. I can literally walk around in a total daze, oblivious to most anything going on around me. The "demons" seem to be in total control during those times!

Years ago I would be this way for days or even weeks at a time. Now when I feel this way, I try to remind myself about all the wonderful things I have in my life and all the things I have accomplished. I also think about how I am not alone. There are a lot of people who love and support me. I try to think about all of the wonderful students I have taught over the years and how much they have meant to me. I think about my family and how much I love them. I think about how successful my children are as adults. I try to counter what the "demons" are saying to me by remembering all the wonderful positive things I have experienced. I keep repeating verbally and visualizing over and over the good things in my life. Usually this works after a while and I may be depressed for only a few days at a time.

**Surround yourself with positive-oriented people.** I try my best to only associate myself with successful, positive people. I stay away from people who radiate negative energy. When I am around people who spread harmful gossip, I instantly feel the negative vibes come back in me. When I am around such people I usually find a way to excuse myself and get away as fast as I can.

**Don't be afraid to speak up.** I have a very hard time standing up to my convictions when challenged. This is one concept I am STILL working on, although I have made considerable progress over the years. Standing up for my beliefs is the same as standing up to a fight. After all the failed attempts I made at standing up to my abusers while growing up, standing up to anybody for any reason, even a mere verbal confrontation, is still the most difficult task for me.

Now, I try to evaluate a situation as it occurs. I consider what would be the *worst* thing that could happen to me if I decide to verbally enter a disagreement. Once I look at the worst case scenario and consider the possible outcomes, I usually go ahead and join in on the argument. Most of the time little to nothing could happen to me in doing so. This tactic helps me to put situations in proper perspective and realize they're not truly extreme threats.

**Get moving!** I try to exercise regularly. Exercise is one of the best ways to overcome depression. Usually once I start exercising I begin to feel better within a few hours. Whenever I start to get depressed I try to find a way to get moving like walking, even if it is only in the office area where I teach. I try to run two to four miles four days a week and circuit train three days a week. In my case, I exercise also to help keep my heart arrhythmia in check. For me, both exercise and medication help to keep my heart stabilized for longer periods of time before it slips back into arrhythmia.

**It's not your fault.** Because of my past experiences, I tend to take everything very personally. It does not matter where or what it is at the moment. If I perceive negative thoughts, implications, or comments coming my way, I instantly assume it was my fault. It does not matter whether I'm at a faculty meeting or working with my students or other professional musicians, I tend to assume everything that went wrong was my fault. Because of my past torment, the "demons" are always ready to bounce on me and begin their dirty work. This is something I've had to work continually to try to correct. Whenever I start to feel negative assumptions, I try to calm myself and rationalize what is really going on. Usually after a few minutes, I begin to calm down and realize that they are not attacking me personally. After evaluating the situation I start to feel better and am usually fine.

**Remember that God loves you.** God loves me and God loves you! When all else fails I always know that no matter what, God will always love me. When I am in my darkest moments of life, I always know that God is there ready to cover me, protect me, and shield me.

# Chapter 21
# God's Purpose for All of Us

God has a different plan for each of us, a plan outlined for you before you were even born. Everybody's journey will be different, and no one else is meant for your journey. That pathway is for you and you alone. We usually do not know where our journey will take us until we are there and look back. If you trust in God, He will lead and empower you, and you will eventually succeed in finding your purpose and His plan for you. God intends for us to use our gifts along life's path. If you are not sure of what your gifts are, reflect on your life. Try things that interest you. Through reflection and possibly new experiences, you will learn what God's plan is for you.

When my wife and I give concerts and personal testimonies about our lives, many people come up to us and talk about how they do not have any special talents. But after talking with them for a few minutes they begin to realize that they too have talents. It could be the love of cooking, coaching, sewing, or babysitting. Once they realize that these too are considered a talent or gift, then they begin to see the larger picture. Everybody enjoys doing something. What do you enjoy doing that you consider fun and even relaxing? That could be your talent or gift, or an avenue toward finding your talent that God has given you to use as a vehicle to spread His love.

I used to want to perform more than being a teacher. It has been interesting to see over the years how God has directed my life in that regard. As for teaching, God has opened unlimited doors of opportunity for me to teach over the years. I even had flutists knock on my hotel room door wanting lessons when I was on the road as a professional musician. They had heard me practicing in the hotel room. As a performer He opens just enough doors to help satisfy my hunger to perform but not enough to interfere with my teaching. Over the last few years I began to realize that my "talent" is being a teacher. I have taught literally thousands of students over the years. Many of them now follow me through Facebook. I feel like they are all my "children."

# Chapter 22
# My Final Thoughts

Currently, my heart still goes in and out of arrhythmia at times. Some days are a lot worse than others. I foresee that within the next year or two, I will probably have my fourth ablation surgery. All I can do is hope that it will work. My other health issues bother me daily. Many times it is still difficult for me to get up for work. As I get older, these issues are getting more and more severe.

I now realize that this is what I have to work with. This is as good as it gets for me. Even with the many health issues I have, I also know how much worse it could be. I am very thankful for what health I have. I am still able to accomplish a lot in life despite my health issues.

So what have I learned? I have learned to use my past to push me forward. Now I take the negative energy of "the demons always screaming at me" and convert it to positive energy to achieve anything I try to do. The louder they are screaming at me, the harder I work until I have achieved success. Now I am an over achiever. I give one-hundred percent to everything I do because of my past.

I have to be very careful not to go into a destructive tailspin. With my heart arrhythmia, it can happen very easily. I have to remind myself all the time that I can do "whatever" despite what the "demons" say. I realized early on that music could be the ticket for me to achieve success in life. Music was my ticket for beating the "demons." Music saved my life. Without music I could not have gained the strength to fight my past. I would not be here today without it. But of course it is God who gave me the gift of music, and God has been with me through all these years.

I now realize that God's purpose for me is to teach music, to help all who I touch to become a better person, and to help show God's love through my music. Now, I proudly wear my abuse as a symbol of my survival.

# Resources

American Heart Association. "Why Atrial Fibrillation (AF or AFib) Matters." *American Heart Association.* May 30, 2012. Web. March 24, 2014.

Averill, Farah. "How Do Bullies Become Bullies?" *Askmen.* AskMen -- Men's Online Magazine. Web. February 28, 2014.

Babbel, Susanne. "The Lingering Trauma of Child Abuse." *Psychology Today.* April 23, 2011. Web. February 12, 2014.

Barkley, Russell A., and Kevin R. Murphy. *Attention Deficit Hyperactivity Disorder: A Clinical Workbook.* 3rd ed. New York: Guilford Press, 2006. Print.

Ellis, Marie. "Bullying Affects Children's Long-Term Health, Study Shows." *Medical News Today.* February 17, 2014. Web. March 5, 2014.

Gordon, Sherri. "10 Reasons Why Kids Are Bullied." *About.com.* Web. March 12, 2014.

Gregg, Valerie R. "When Abused Children Grow Up." *Emory Medicine.* Emory University, Summer 1999. Web. March 15, 2014.

Mahfood, Julie. "Bullying Victims' Long-Term Health." *Guardian Liberty Voice.* February 18, 2014. Web. March 15, 2014.

Mayo Clinic Staff. "Heart Arrhythmia" *Mayo Clinic.* February 27, 2013. Web. March 24, 2014.

Melloy, Kilian. "Your Brain on Bullying." *Edge Boston.* March 21, 2011. Web. March 15, 2014.

Rettner, Rachael. "Bullies on Bullying: Why We Do It." *Live Science*. August 26, 2010. Web. February 25, 2014.

St. Clair, Janet. "What Causes Bullies?" *By Parents-For Parents*. 2011. Web. March 14, 2014.

Sognonvi, Serge, and Carmen Sognonvi. "Why Do Bullies Bully? The Top 5 Reasons Why People Bully Others." *Urbandojo.com*. June 16, 2010. Web. February 28, 2014.

Why do People Bully? Retrieved February 28, 2014, from http://www.bullyingstatistics.org/content/why-do-people-bully.html.

www.ingramcontent.com/pod-product-compliance
Lightning Source LLC
LaVergne TN
LVHW011354080426
835511LV00005B/288